To Drink and To Eat

Tastes & Techniques
from a
French Kitchen

THE CULINARY MEMOIR
OF A MODERN YOUNG MAN

X DRINK X EAT

To Drink and To Eat

Tastes & Techniques from a French Kitchen

— GUILLAUME LONG —

New Edition

Colors Mélanie Roubineau
and Guillaume Long

AN ONI PRESS PUBLICATION

English Translation by Jeremy Melloul
Lettering by AndWorld Design's D.C. Hopkins
Colors by Guillaume Long, Mélanie Roubleau, and Céline Badarous Denizon
Cover Art by Guillaume Long
Design by Annie Monette
New Edition Design by Sonja Synak
Editing and Localization by Amanda Meadows and Grace Bornhoft

Published by Oni-Lion Forge Publishing Group, LLC.

James Lucas Jones, president & publisher
Sarah Gaydos, editor in chief
Charlie Chu, e.v.p. of creative & business development
Brad Rooks, director of operations
Amber O'Neill, special projects manager
Harris Fish, events manager
Margot Wood, director of marketing & sales
Jeremy Atkins, director of brand communications
Devin Funches, sales & marketing manager
Tara Lehmann, marketing & publicity associate
Troy Look, director of design & production
Kate Z. Stone, senior graphic designer
Sonja Synak, graphic designer
Hilary Thompson, graphic designer

Angie Knowles, digital prepress lead
Shawna Gore, senior editor
Robin Herrera, senior editor
Amanda Meadows, senior editor
Jasmine Amiri, editor
Grace Bornhoft, editor
Zack Soto, editor
Steve Ellis, director of games
Ben Eisner, game developer
Michelle Nguyen, executive assistant
Jung Lee, logistics coordinator

Joe Nozemack, publisher emeritus

1319 SE Martin Luther King, Jr. Blvd.
Suite 240
Portland, OR 97214

onipress.com | lionforge.com

facebook.com/onipress | facebook.com/lionforge

twitter.com/onipress | twitter.com/lionforge

instagram.com/onipress | instagram.com/lionforge

lemonde.fr/blog/long
facebook.com/0c0ABAM
twitter.com/0c0ABAM
instagram.com/0c0ABAM

First Edition: February 2020
ISBN: 978-1-62010-720-1

Library Congress Control Number: 2019945813

Printed in China.

This book is dedicated to all the people with whom I shared a pleasant moment over drinks or a good meal.

—G. L.

Foreword

To my dearest and most talented friend, Guillaume:

Thank you, *mon ami*, for recognizing me as your most ardent fan and friend in the US. And, for gifting me this precious opportunity to preview your, frankly speaking, fucking spectacular book. It gives me warm feels in my soul to see that you followed in my footsteps and *also* published a really creative memoir cookbook. *Bravo* to the both of us!

It's been a while, but life falls through the cracks, so I don't take it personally at all. Admittedly, I wasn't incredibly fond of the hassle your book people put me through, but after indulging in the visual culinary brilliance of your book, I was put at (incredibly hunger-inducing) ease.

I hate to admit this to you, but my limited childhood exposure to France was disappointingly from TV reruns of *Bon Voyage Charlie Brown* (btw, your David Lynch and Kubrick references are so cool!); a Toblerone chocolate my Parisian Uncle gifted me once (that I now know is from Switzerland... and you can get it at ANY 7-Eleven, as pointed out by my 7-Eleven managing mom), which could work for the "sagging" – your book's words not mine – chocolate cake recipe.

I'm only able to read *To Drink and to Eat* sparingly in the moments of peace between life's most chaotic orchestral movements and the quietest recesses of bodily necessity we all succumb to... OK, I read this exclusively on the toilet. Not because that's where it belongs and thrives best, but because I'm busy and it's the only place where I can't cook and my kid bothers me less. But it's the best of toilet times. You may say c'est la vie, but I prefer, "sorry, not sorry." :p

Guillaume, you illustrate hilarious autobiographical portrayals of your gastronomic experiences, and obsession with kitchen tools (that Princess Leia hair bun'ed Spirelli'ed cat hit both my geek and funny bones, *mwahaha*)! The simple admission that you get lazy drawing when it gets hot is as compelling a page turner as it gets. Your insight on the variety of food you've made and eaten, from life in France to your jealousy-inducing travels to Italy, Hungary, and all the delicious countries you have afforded yourself to explore and draw beautifully, is an absolute wonderful journey to partake in – even the crappy places! By the way, is the Swiss-Chinese restaurant you visited a direct challenge to me? Either way, I accept! I will try this "laminar salad" and check out the local "junkies" who almost beat you up because you sketched them while eating. What have I told you before—"Restraint, Guillaume. RESTRAINT!"

Truly, I'm proud of what you have given the world and sing your praises (and recipes)! I will scribe lyrics from your recipes, even though you already did for your eggs. *To Drink and to Eat* will be how I test my friendships with the temptation to steal your tasty tome of food humor and wisdom from me. If they love your work as much as I do, I couldn't completely fault them for being savages. After I completely sever ties with them, and blacklist them from my restaurant and my infamous (Crispy Tofu) balls, of course.

You tease my curiosity and appetite with your stories of the black radish, the comic fish compendium, your tomato bible, and THE SARDINIAN TOMATOES… the way you describe them makes me cry and drool all at once. No more overlooking my emails, let's make that trip to Sardinia, pretty please! I loved how you included your most charming family in your almost-too-saccharine-for-me semi-charmed life (I knew they looked familiar, Oh Pépé!). Also, your culinary life lessons from our beloved friends (though not me, sad face), and fictional-but-admittedly-cute culinary bureaucrat characters make this such a fun read.

Why didn't we work together on my first book, *Adventures in Starry Kitchen*? Think of what could have been! Now look at you, peacocking your mind-bogglingly concise dinner party tips for the world to entertain company, while I'm instructing people to start a restaurant career illegally! Let's collaborate on the next one? (Or, if Nancy's available, that'd be AWESOME, because her drawing makes me wonder who the real talent is.)

Let's catch up soon. Life doesn't have the warning signs that we need and want, like in "The Promise" (my favorite moments in the book), but I have a feeling if you had your way… you'd get a snazzy air conditioner for drawing on hot days. Then you won't have to draw yourself in underwear! You'd also become less lazy for your editors… but then again, that might stifle the humor and pizzazz that makes your comics special.

Oh, hey! After all the hassle, looks like I convinced your convivial publisher to run my foreword in your new edition of *To Drink and to Eat*! I can't think of anyone better for the task. Who else can sell you, to people neither you nor I know and paint a culinary canvas of colorful comic excitement, hunger, hiliarity, cross-country Italian coffee maker lovin', and, *ahem*, JOËL ROBUCHON TIPS (wait a sec, why didn't you ever introduce us?).

Bises to Nancy, Pépé Roni, and the rest of the Guillaume gastronomic group!

Eternally yours… and hungry,

Nguyen Tran—

    Chief Instigating Officer, (The Adventures in) Starry Kitchen

PS: Who is that chef friend you constantly swim with and get tips from, who obviously isn't me? And why not?! I think my banana suit would fit in nicely?

[Author's note: Nguyen and I have never met. —G.L.]

Contents

Manual

 Level 1: Recipes requiring no cooking experience. Quick, with no actual cooking involved.

 Level 2: Recipes that are slightly more involved, take some time, and require some cooking.

 Level 3: Recipes that are very difficult to make (only sometimes; I'm mainly joking).

 Egotrip: Stories about myself.

 Restaurant: Stories of meals in places I like.

 Inventory: Useful lists for foodies.

 Joël Reblochon: Cooking tips and history presented by the late Joël Reblochon.

 New Friend: Cooking commentary provided by my friend Florian.

 Leftovers: Everything that doesn't fit in one of the other categories in this book.

Spring

The new apron

leon.

One Sunday morning, I was listening to Rebecca Manzoni interview Jean-Pierre Bacri on the radio, and I remembered an anecdote from my childhood:

No, but...it pisses me off...all this promotion...I mean...isn't it annoying?

When I was seven or eight years old, and I had yet to develop an allergy to grasses, I was plucking seeds from the lawn.

I don't know if it was because they looked like cereal, but one day I had the bright idea to make a bread out of them.

My grandma, who was watching me for the day, helped me in this endeavor which, to this day, is the first recipe I remember creating.

We let the result of our work bake while I played in my room during the afternoon.

My bread, all warm and fresh out of the oven, was a great hit and my mom praised me for it.

Years later, I learned that the bread I had made had been thrown away and replaced with a rye bread from the local bakery. They had put it in the oven for a few minutes so I wouldn't be any wiser.

That Sunday, this is what Bacri said: "When you're a child, you draw something and your mother says, 'Ooh, that's great!'"

"You've drawn a total mess with a red marker, but your mother says, 'Mmm, you did a great job.'"

Well!

Looks good, right?

"And you spend the rest of your life chasing after that feeling."

lon.

A GOOD COFFEE

MAKING GOOD COFFEE? HMM, THAT'S A BIG QUESTION THAT DESERVES ITS OWN BOOK...

BUT I'LL TRY TO BREAK IT DOWN.

SLRRRP.

WHERE TO START? LET'S SEE... YOU NEED COFFEE, OF COURSE. AND WATER. A FLYSWATTER AND, MOST IMPORTANTLY, A COFFEE MAKER.

CA. FÉ

A **REAL** ONE.

FORGET ABOUT NESPRESSO® AND THE OTHER FAKERS...

TCHIII

THEY MIGHT BE COOL AND PRODUCE DECENT COFFEE, BUT THEY ALL TASTE THE SAME.

AND DROP THE FANTASY OF SOMEDAY HAVING A CONA COFFEE MAKER.

FWIP FWIP

THEY'RE OVERKILL-- AND WAY TOO EXPENSIVE. THE TYPE OF THING YOU ONLY USE ONCE.

AS FOR YOUR ELECTRIC COFFEE MAKER, SELL IT OR JUST THROW IT AWAY. THEY'RE SO UGLY.

KRR-RRR

WHAT A HORRIBLE SOUND

THE COFFEE THAT IT MAKES IS SAD AND, IF YOU'RE NOT AWARE, CAUSES ABSCESSES BETWEEN YOUR TOES.

IGNORE YOUR BODUM ®, TOO.

...

BECAUSE... WELL, JUST TRUST ME. AND ANYWAY, MAKING GOOD COFFEE REQUIRES A HEALTHY DOSE OF SUPERSTITION.

YOU CAN START BY GETTING...

An Italian Coffee Maker

DECORATION →

LID

TUBE (2)

(EXCELLENT) COFFEE

ERGONOMIC HANDLE

FILTER (2)

NO HYPER-RESISTANT SCREWS

GROUND COFFEE

FILTER (1)

SAFETY VALVE

TUBE (1)

BOILING WATER

(UNNECESSARY SECTIONAL VIEW OF POT FOR EFFECT.)

I HAVE THREE AT HOME:

FOUR CUPS, SIX YEARS OLD

SIX CUPS, THREE YEARS OLD

SIX CUPS, NEWBORN

I LOVE THEM; I SPOIL THEM. I COULD'VE PROBABLY EVEN NAMED THEM...

FOR SOME PEOPLE IT'S CARS, FOR ME IT'S COFFEE MAKERS.

THE POINT IS TO HAVE ONE FOR THE REST OF YOUR LIFE... OVER TIME, THE COFFEE IT MAKES BECOMES EVEN MORE DELICIOUS...

SO, MAKE YOUR CHOICE CAREFULLY.

IF ONLY I HAD KNOWN!

HELL OF A BREW.

FOR COFFEE, IT'S DIFFERENT... ESSENTIALLY, YOU'VE GOT A CHOICE BETWEEN:

WILD

DOMESTICATED

ARABICA (BELIEVED TO BE THE BEST)

ROBUSTA (MORE POPULAR)

AND WITHIN THESE TWO CATEGORIES THERE ARE HUNDREDS OF DIFFERENT VARIETIES!

SO, FIND THE COFFEE THAT INTERESTS YOU, TASTE IT, AND TEST!

I PREFER ARABICA'S.

A MOKA, TO BE PRECISE:

The Yirgacheffe from Ethiopia

IT'S HARD TO FIND, TRUE. COARSE, PUNGENT, AND TASTES OF DIRT AND CHOCOLATE...

WHAT A COFFEE!

IF YOU CAN, BUY YOUR COFFEE AT A COFFEE ROASTERS: THEY'LL GIVE YOU ADVICE AND GRIND IT FOR YOUR COFFEE MAKER.

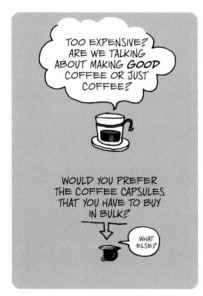

TOO EXPENSIVE? ARE WE TALKING ABOUT MAKING **GOOD** COFFEE OR JUST COFFEE?

WOULD YOU PREFER THE COFFEE CAPSULES THAT YOU HAVE TO BUY IN BULK?

WHAT ELSE?

GOOOD... NOW YOU ARE READY FOR...

ZE COFFEE!

IF IT'S YOUR FIRST TIME USING AN ITALIAN COFFEE MAKER, YOU'LL HAVE TO MAKE AT LEAST **THREE** COFFEES FIRST.

SO THAT THE COFFEE MAKER LOSES THAT "NEW" TASTE.

IF YOU'RE ALREADY USING ONE, **BUT** YOU AREN'T FOLLOWING THE EIGHT POINTS BELOW TO THE LETTER...

IT'S NOT TOO LATE!

1 FILL THE LOWER PART OF THE COFFEE MAKER WITH WATER.

UNTIL IT REACHES THE VALVE

ATTACH THE FILTER LIKE SO:

2 FILL THE FILTER WITH COFFEE, BUT DON'T PACK IT IN TOO TIGHTLY! WE WANT THE WATER TO RISE.

FOR THE PROPORTIONS, IT'S UP TO YOU. ME, I PREFER MY COFFEE STRONG, SO I FILL THE FILTER TO THE BRIM.

3 SCREW IN THE TOP PART OF THE COFFEE MAKER. DON'T FORCE IT, BUT MAKE SURE IT'S SECURE...

...AND THEN HEAT IT UP.

4 KEEP AN EYE ON YOUR COFFEE.

IT'S IMPORTANT.

AND THE FIRE, TOO.

NO   YES   NO

NB: IF YOU ONLY HAVE AN ELECTRIC PLATE, WELL... I DON'T KNOW, DO WHAT YOU WANT... THAT'S ALREADY PUNISHMENT ENOUGH.

IT...IT HURTS.

HEH, YES.

BUT GOOD COFFEE TAKES TIME.

SSSSCRRCHHRRCR

AH!

DO YOU HEAR **THAT!?**

5 THE "SCRRRCLLCHRLER" SOUND YOUR COFFEE MAKER IS MAKING IS YOUR SIGN TO REDUCE THE HEAT, OR CUT OUT THE FIRE ENTIRELY, IMMEDIATELY WHILE THE COFFEE FINISHES RAISING.

IF YOU DON'T, THE JOINT AND THE BASE WILL BURN.

(HELLO, AFTERTASTE.)

AND IT'S READY!

6 IF YOU WANT GOOD COFFEE, YOU HAVE TO TAKE GOOD CARE OF YOUR COFFEE MAKER.

NO DISHWASHING PRODUCTS   NO ROUGH SPONGES   JUST WATER

I NEVER WASH THE BOTTOM OF THE COFFEE MAKER (WHICH, OVER TIME, MATURES AND GIVES YOUR COFFEE DEPTH OF FLAVOR), BUT I DO RINSE IT REGULARLY.

FOR THE TOP PART, I CLEAN IT WITH WATER AND THE SOFT SIDE OF A SPONGE ONCE PER MONTH.

7 IF YOU'RE LAZY, GOOD NEWS: **DON'T THROW AWAY** THE COFFEE THAT'S BEEN FILTERED THROUGH YOUR COFFEE MAKER.

(EXCEPT IF YOU ONLY MAKE IT ONCE PER MONTH, AND YOU SEE FOAM ON THE JOINT.)

THIS WAY, THE COFFEE YOU MAKE IN THAT COFFEE MAKER WILL GRADUALLY LOSE ITS METALLIC TASTE.

TO EMPTY THE FILTER:

 PUF!

 TAP!

8 THE LAST **ESSENTIAL** POINT:

TO MAKE A REALLY GOOD COFFEE, IF NOT THE BEST (AND THIS ADVICE STILL STANDS **EVEN** IF YOU'RE USING AN ELECTRIC COFFEE MAKER) WATCH OUT FOR ABSCESSES.

YOU HAVE TO BELIEVE YOU'RE MAKING THE BEST COFFEE.

AND I'M BEING **REALLY** SERIOUS!

MY TECHNIQUE INVOLVES SAYING:

HERE IS THE COFFEE! LET ME JUST TELL YOU THAT IT'S THE BEST IN JURA!*

I'M NOT MESSING AROUND!

AND AS A RESULT, I'M CONVINCED THAT IN JURA (THOUGH THERE AREN'T THAT MANY PEOPLE HERE), MY COFFEE WILL BE THE BEST. I KNOW IT.

IT'S WORKING!   WOW   IT REALLY IS GOOD.   MMMH

*WHERE I LIVE

IF YOU LIVE IN PARIS, LIMIT YOURSELF TO YOUR ARRONDISSEMENT TO SEEM MORE REALISTIC...

THIS IS THE BEST COFFEE IN THE 20TH...

WOOOOO   IT'S WORKING!

BUT IN ICELAND, DON'T WORRY ABOUT IT:

LET ME TELL YOU   DAGRÜT!*

*WE DON'T CARE, WE'RE COLD, GIVE IT!

NOW **OBVIOUSLY,** THERE'S **ALWAYS** SOME CLEVER PERSON WHO ASKS:

SLRP

NOT BAD, BUT DO YOU HAVE ANY SUGAR?

THAT'S WHAT THE FLYSWATTER IS FOR.

AIM FOR THE TIP OF THE NOSE: YOU NEVER PUT SUGAR IN COFFEE (OR IN TEA).

lon.

ASIDE

IN *MULHOLLAND DRIVE* BY DAVID LYNCH, THERE'S A TENSE SCENE WHERE WE SEE PEOPLE NEGOTIATE A CONTRACT FOR A MOVIE.

THEN, AT ONE POINT, A GUY (LUIGI) ORDERS A COFFEE, AND WE CAN TELL HE'S NOT HERE TO MESS AROUND:

ESPRESSO

NAPKIN

HE TAKES A SINGLE SIP, AND THEN HE STARTS SPITTING IT OUT INTO HIS NAPKIN!

HE SAYS:

IT'S SHIT!!

AND HE:

FLPFLPF

AND THEN HE GETS UP, EXTREMELY ANGRY. THE MEETING IS RUINED, AND THE TWO GUYS (RAY AND MR. DARBY) START TO APOLOGIZE:

I'M SORRY

THAWASHIGHLY RECOMM--

WHICH PROVES TWO THINGS:

1) IF YOU'RE NOT USING AN ITALIAN COFFEE MAKER, THEN YOU'RE MAKING CRAPPY COFFEE!

PIECE OF SHIT!

2) IF THE TWO GUYS HAD SAID THAT IT WAS THE BEST COFFEE IN THE WORLD (NOT ONE OF THE BEST, BUT THE BEST!) ***BEFORE*** SERVING THE COFFEE, WELL I BET THAT LUIGI WOULD'VE LOVED IT!

BUT THE SCENE WOULDN'T HAVE BEEN AS INTERESTING...

LYNCH KNEW.

lon.

Pépé Roni's Good Advice: skimming

n° 278

You can't confuse "skimming over the ocean"

and "skimming a soup."

BECAUSE ANYONE CAN MAKE MISTAKES!

Skimming: Removing, with the help of a skimmer, the foam or scum that forms on the surface of a dish when it is cooked.

YOU PLAYED WITH IT WHEN YOU WERE A CHILD.

YOU BARELY PAY ATTENTION TO IT IN THE STREET.

YOU SEE IT FROM TIME TO TIME FROM YOUR CAR.

Dandelions, are a little like life...

I am poetry

In springtime, they symbolize hope and renewal for us...

AND NOW YOU'RE GOING TO EAT IT!

AND NOT BY THE ROOTS!

HE HE!

THE DANDELION

But its bitterness is a good reminder of how hard life can be sometimes....

EW!

MHM HM

And that you need to season it properly if you want to appreciate it.

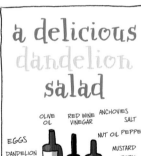

a delicious dandelion salad

OLIVE OIL
RED WINE VINEGAR
ANCHOVIES
SALT
EGGS
NUT OIL PEPPER
DANDELION FLOWERS
MUSTARD
PORK BELLY

1 GATHER SOME DANDELIONS, BUT BE CAREFUL: ONLY THE YOUNG ONES THAT HAVE YET TO FLOWER (IN OTHER WORDS, HARVEST THE ONES THAT ARE TENDER).

WELL, THIS WON'T MAKE A PRETTY BOUQUET.

MOM!

NEMO!

2 THIS IS THE LONGEST AND MOST ANNOYING PART: CAREFULLY WASH THE LEAVES, SORT THEM, AND REMOVE THE ROOTS.

YOU CAN KEEP THE BULBS

FINALLY, SOAK THEM FOR FIVE MINUTES IN A BASIN OF WATER WITH TWO TABLESPOONS OF VINEGAR.

IT KILLS MICROBES.

OF COURSE, STEPS (1) AND (2) ARE USELESS IF YOU'RE BUYING YOUR DANDELIONS. BUT WHY WOULD YOU PAY FOR BAD HERBS (ESPECIALLY WHEN THEY'RE USUALLY EXPENSIVE)?

YEAH, BUT I'M USED TO THE CITY.

I'M NOT GOING ALL THE WAY TO THE COUNTRY JUST FOR DANDELIONS.

3 MAKE SOME HARD-BOILED EGGS (ONE PER PERSON IS GOOD).

WAIT EXACTLY NINE MINUTES

OPEN UP A BOX OF ANCHOVIES.

OR FRY THE SMOKED PORK BELLY IN SLICES.

TSHH!

4 PREPARE A SPICY VINAIGRETTE TO BALANCE THE DANDELION SALAD'S BITTERNESS.

THEY'RE FAR MORE BITTER THAN PINE NUTS EXCEPT THAT THE AFTERTASTE DOESN'T LAST A WEEK.

FOR EVERY TWO SPOONS OF OIL (OLIVE OR OTHERWISE), ADD HALF AS MUCH MUSTARD, TWO SPOONS OF VINEGAR, ONE SPOON OF NUT OIL, AND SALT AND PEPPER.

5 MIX THE SALAD TOGETHER AND TASTE IT:

KRRRRK DAMN!

IT'S SO BITTER.

AND, IF NEEDED, ADD A LITTLE BIT OF NORMAL SALAD, EVEN IF IT'S LESS "GREEN."

LET'S KICK SOME BUTT!

6 ON A PLATE, DRESS THE SALAD, AND SPRINKLE SOME GRILLED PORK OR ANCHOVIES, OR BOTH.

WOOO, FATTY!!

THEN TOP WITH AN EGG, CUT IN FOUR:

IT REALLY IS BITTER.

OR IS IT JUST ME?

ALL THOSE ANCHO-VIES.

leon.

Marinate: Soaking a food item into a marinade to tenderize it and give it flavor.

A WHILE AGO, MY CHERISHED DARLING GOT ME A--

WHAT IS IT?

OPEN IT, YOU'LL SEE!

A NABAZTAG®?

BETTER.

BUT IT'S TOO SMALL TO BE A PROJECTOR IN THE SHAPE OF R2D2?

OH COOL...

UH... WHAT IS IT?

A GARLIC MILL

COOL

WELL, THANKS!

I GUESS FOR CHRISTMAS I'LL GET YOU AN AIR CONDITIONING UNIT...

IF THESE ARE THE KINDS OF GIFTS WE'RE GIVING!

THE GARLIC MILL STAYED UNUSED FOR A LONG TIME IN ITS CORNER OF THE KITCHEN. I COULD FEEL IT TAUNTING ME EVERY TIME I MINCED GARLIC.

TCHAC TCHAC TCHAC

THEN, ONE DAY, I TRIED IT.

DAMN IT, HOW DOES THIS WORK...

IT'S GOING TO TAKE ME THREE HOURS TO CLEAN...

HANDLE

PLASTIC

TRANSPARENT

SPRING

PRESS

GARLIC

BLADES

WELL, I THINK I EXPERIENCED WHAT PREHISTORIC MAN FELT WHEN THEY FIRST DISCOVERED TOOLS:

FLOP FLOP FLOP FLOP FLOP FLOP FLOP FLOP

WOOOAH!

PRECISION

FINESSE

SPEED

SHAVINGS

THE GARLIC MILL SOON TOOK CENTER STAGE IN MY KITCHEN...

STANDING PROUDLY ALONGSIDE ITS FELLOW STARS...

TODAY, I USE IT OFTEN.

SOMETIMES *TOO* OFTEN.

WE'RE BEST FRIENDS FOREVER.

WHEN I WAS A KID, MY FAVORITE MAGAZINE TO READ WAS *ASTRAPI*, AND I HAVE ONE MEMORY IN PARTICULAR FROM AN ISSUE OF THE MAGAZINE ALL ABOUT:

THE **BREADED FISH**

THE ARTICLE, WHICH WAS WRITTEN QUITE SERIOUSLY, EXPLAINED THE LIFE OF THIS CURIOUS FISH:

THE WAY IT HIDES IN THE SAND

THE EYE THAT GAVE IT AWAY

AND THAT THE FISHERMAN REMOVED

AND ITS SKIN, WHICH YOU HAD TO CLEAN

AS A RESULT, I NEVER LIKED THAT FISH. IT ALWAYS SEEMED A LITTLE "OFF" TO ME. INSTEAD, I PREFERRED FISH THAT WERE MORE "NATURAL" WITH SCALES, BONES, AND A REAL STENCH...

IT WASN'T UNTIL YEARS LATER WHEN I WAS GOING THROUGH OLD BOXES THAT I CAME ACROSS THAT ISSUE AGAIN AND REALIZED THAT IT WAS PUBLISHED ON APRIL 1ST.

NOOO!

DAMN AND THE LITTLE MOUSE, TOO!

HOLY COW...

TODAY, *ASTRAPI* STILL EXISTS, AND I STILL THINK BREADED FISH IS DISGUSTING. I WONDER IF THEY STILL MAKE THE SAME JOKE IN APRIL AND IF IT CONTINUES TO SAVE CHILDREN FROM THAT DREADED FISH.

len.

Pépé Roni's Good Advice: a peeler   n° 599

Don't confuse a "skinflint"

and a "skin peeler."

BECAUSE ANYONE CAN MAKE MISTAKES!

A skin peeler: A paring knife with which you can peel the skins off of vegetables and fruits.

YOU TOOK YOUR NISSAN PATROL©, YOUR QUECHUA TENT©, YOUR VICTORINOX© SWISS KNIFE, DRESSED IN YOUR CAMEL TROPHY EXPLORER'S OUTFIT. AND EVEN AN RPG-7 YOU FOUND ON EBAY© THAT'S IN YOUR TRUNK.

BEAR'S GARLIC

I... I DID IT!

ALL BECAUSE, FOR THE FIRST TIME, YOU'RE GOING TO GATHER RAMSONS--OR BEAR'S GARLIC--AND BECAUSE, IN YOUR MIND, YOU THINK IT'LL BE LIKE:

SO, IT'S A LITTLE SHOCKING WHEN YOU REALIZE THAT YOU CAN ACTUALLY FIND RAMSONS IN ALMOST ANY UNDERGROWTH IN LARGE QUANTITIES:

OH WOW.

ACTUALLY, YOU CAN EVEN PAY A LOT OF MONEY TO BUY 3.5 OZ WORTH AT THE LOCAL ORGANIC GROCERY STORE:

YEAH, YEAH WE GET IT!

SHEESH.

YOU DECIDE TO TRY TO MAKE A NUTRITIOUS PUREE FOR YOUR SON.

TCHAC TCHAC TCHAC TCHAC

UNFORTUNATELY: YOU CONFUSE RAMSONS WITH LILY OF THE VALLEY (EXTREMELY POISONOUS):

NO, DON'T ...

100 Toxic Plants

YUMM SLURRP

OKAY, WELL AT LEAST YOUR SECOND TRY AT THE SOUP IS BOUND TO BE A SUCCESS WITH YOUR WIFE:

HONEY, I'VE GOT TO TELL YOU SOMETHING...

BUT LET'S EAT FIRST!

OH, UH, SORRY! YOU DIDN'T KNOW THAT COLCHICUM HAD THE SAME LEAVES, BUT JUST IN A LARGER SIZE?

THIS IS STARTING TO BE A LITTLE MUCH JUST FOR AN AROMATIC HERB...

DAMN BEAR'S GARLIC

WELL, IT'S ALL RIGHT. YOU CAN FIND SOME ACTUAL BEAR'S GARLIC PICKED BY PEOPLE WHO KNOW WHAT THEY'RE DOING FOR SALE AT A REALLY HIGH PRICE AT THE LOCAL ORGANIC MARKET.

AH, BEAR'S GARLIC! YES, YOU REALLY SHOULDN'T GET IT WRONG... I MEAN, WELL, IT DOES SMELL OF GARLIC WHEN YOU CRUSH IT, AND IT COVERS THE UNDERGROWTHS WITH SMALL WHITE FLOWERS.

OH, SPEAKING OF... ARE YOU SURE THERE'S NO RISK OF ECHINOCOCCOSIS WHERE YOU--

ECHINO-CO-WHAT?

I... I...

SHEESH, THIS KOUNEN BROTHERS FILM ISN'T GREAT...

BEAR'S GARLIC IS REALLY GOOD AND NOT THAT COMPLICATED TO PREPARE SAFELY-- LIKE IN A PESTO, FOR EXAMPLE...

FOR A Bear's Garlic Pesto

(1) YOU NEED A HANDFUL OF HERBS YOU'VE WASHED **VERY** WELL.

THEN YOU PUT THEM IN A POT OF BOILING WATER, FOR ONE OR TWO MINUTES.

FLPFLOP

(3) ONCE YOU'VE DRAINED THEM AS MUCH AS POSSIBLE, YOU MIX THE LEAVES WITH OLIVE OIL:

BVV VRVV VRR

WHICH SHOULD GIVE YOU A SORT OF SLIGHTLY LIQUID, GREEN PASTE WHICH YOU SEASON WITH SALT AND PEPPER.

(2) THEN YOU DRAIN IT AND RINSE WITH COLD WATER AND ICE CUBES TO STOP THE LEAVES FROM COOKING AND TO HELP SET THE COLOR OF THE LEAVES:

AND THAT'S IT! YOU CAN KEEP IT IN THE FRIDGE FOR A WEEK, AND YOU CAN PUT IT IN PASTA, A RISOTTO, OR A SALAD!

AND IT'S DELI-CIOUS!

SEE YOU NEXT TIME, AND BON APPÉTIT!

Flowers

Stem

Leaves

Bulbs

Bear's garlic

lon.

YOU'RE PROBABLY PART OF THE

52%

OF FRENCH PEOPLE

WHO BELIEVE THEY EAT TOO MUCH MEAT, IN GENERAL, AND SAY THAT THEY PREFER FISH AND THAT IT'S BETTER FOR THEIR HEALTH.

EXACTLY THE SAME AMOUNT OF PEOPLE WHO ARE AGAINST--

NOW HOLD ON A MINUTE!

THAT'S NOT NORMAL, YOU KNOW!

OR ELSE YOU OPEN THE DOOR TO A LOT OF OTHER THINGS.

AND IT'S TOTALLY NORMAL TO BE AGAINST THAT!

EVEN IF IT HAS **NOTHING** TO DO WITH IT.

HOWEVER, EVEN IF YOU BELONG TO THIS MAJORITY, YOU (BERNARD) DON'T ACT ACCORDINGLY WHEN BUYING GROCERIES.

BECAUSE EVEN THOUGH YOU MIGHT KNOW YOUR STUFF IN THE MEAT SECTION...

BLACK RADISH (?)

12X SAUSAGES

4X PORK BELLY

18X TURKEY LIVERY

BEEF RIB

SALAD

TOILET PAPER

4X GROUND STEAK

IN THE FRESH FISH SECTION...

HERE'S THE TRUTH

OH SHIT, WHAT DO I DO?

ONLY REMEMBERS HOW TO COOK BREADED FISH

FISHMONGER WHO SAW YOU AND IS GOING TO ASK YOU WHAT KIND OF FISH YOU WANT

THE FILETS DANCE A BALLET IN FRONT OF YOU.

RED SNAPPER

CATFISH

BLUEFISH

BASS

POLLOCK

MACKEREL

PIKE

GUPPY

ESCOLAR

DRUM

A THOUSAND DIFFERENT NAMES ALL PRONOUNCED EXOTICALLY!

FOR A SECOND, YOU THINK ABOUT RUNNING AWAY TO THE ORGANIC FOOD AISLE AND BUYING TOFU INSTEAD...

WITH STEAMED BROCCOLI?

WHAT A TREAT!

BUT YOU STILL HAVE YOUR DIGNITY!

FORTUNATELY
A SOLUTION EXISTS

NO MORE HUMILIATION

NO MORE UNKNOWN NAMES

NO MORE MUSTACHE

YOU CAN HOLD YOUR HEAD UP HIGH WITH YOUR FISHMONGER THANKS TO...

MINI GUIDE

TO RECOGNIZING FISH WHEN IT'S NOT IN FISH FORM

AND TO IMPRESSING YOUR

FISHMONGER

"STOP HESITATING, DUDE, GET THAT FISH!"

● POACHED ● FRIED ● STEAMED ● BAKED ● GRILLED ● RAW

HADDOCK

ANCHOVY

WOLFFISH

COD

PLAICE

HAKE

CONGER

BREAM

SMELT

SWORDFISH

FERA

HALIBUT

HERRING

LING

DAB

BURBOT

WHITING

MONKFISH

 WHAT WOULD YOU LIKE?

PERCH

BREADED FISH

RAY

SHARK

RED MULTIPLE — RED MULLET

NURSEHOUND

JOHN DORY

ZANDER

SARDINES

SALMON

ROCKFISH

FLOUNDER

TUNA
(DON'T EAT RED TUNA)

TILAPIA

TROUT

TURBOT

len.

EVERYTHING STARTED THE OTHER DAY, WHEN I WAS BUYING FISH...

HELLO...

I'D LIKE A FILET OF PLAICE... TO... FRY.

HOW IS HE DOING THAT? *WHAT* IS THAT PAPER?

EVERYTHING WAS GOING WELL, AND THEN...

HE SAID THE FOLLOWING:

NO PROBLEM...

ARE YOU GOING TO FLOUR IT?

GOT HIM.

YOU COULD'VE JUST FRIED YOUR FILLET LIKE YOU PLANNED.

BUT YOU HAVE TO ADMIT...

FLOURED FISH IS DELICIOUS.

GRILLED FLOURED FISH

GOLDEN

PEPPER

GRILLED

FAT

TENDER

SALT

TASTY

CRISPY

YOU FIND YOURSELF WITH A FILET IN THE AIR, YOUR HAND READY TO PLUNGE INTO THE FLOUR LIKE AL PACINO IN *SCARFACE* SHOVING HIS FACE INTO A MOUNTAIN OF COKE.

HAHA HAHA!

DON'T FUCK WITH ME!

I'M TONY MONTANA!

WELL, THERE'S A MUCH SIMPLER WAY TO FLOUR A FISH!

THOUGH IT MIGHT BE A LITTLE LESS DRAMATIC.

HAHAHA!

TAKE A RANDOM PLASTIC BAG.

NOT A HUGE ONE.

YOU KNOW, A SMALL ONE LIKE YOU MIGHT FIND IN NATURE...

DRIFTING AWAY FROM THEIR SUPERMARKET HOMES.

THE SMALL ONES LIKE FROM A SUPERMARKET.

THE ONES YOU PAY FOR WHEN YOU FORGET TO BRING YOUR OWN BAGS (TOTALLY YOUR FAULT).

OPEN IT AND PUT A FEW SPOONS OF FLOUR INSIDE.

BUT NOT TOO MUCH.

SEASON THE FISH WITH SALT AND PEPPER, AND PUT IT IN THE BAG!

I HOPE, FOR YOUR SAKE, THAT YOUR BAG DOESN'T HAVE ANY HOLES.

CLOSE THE BAG TIGHTLY, AND THEN SHAKE IT HARD.

GNNY

RUSSIAN TONY MONTANA

FLFL FLFL

AND VOILA. YOU HAVE A BEAUTIFUL FILET, WELL-FLOURED, READY TO FRY, WITHOUT MAKING A MESS OF YOUR KITCHEN.

SHAKE OFF THE EXCESS FLOUR.

FRY IT UP WITH A LITTLE BIT OF FAT.

FCChhhh

PSHII

SOME LEMON TO DELGAZE IT.

AND REUSE THE PLASTIC BAG AS TRASH.

EEEK!

I FOLLOWED ALL THE STEPS, AND I BURNED IT!

I FORGOT: IF YOU'RE USING GROCERY BAGS, MAKE SURE YOU'VE REMOVED THE RECEIPT BEFORE FLOURING YOUR FISH.

AND ENJOY YOUR MEAL!

SHIT... IT BURNS!

leon.

LIFE HASN'T BEEN KIND TO YOU RECENTLY...

HERE YOU ARE, LEFT TO YOUR OWN DEVICES...

Hey, Mom? The last time you came to clean, where did you put my tax files?

WAIT, VIRGINIA! YOU CAN'T DO THIS TO ME!

HEY!

ALONE

BUT THAT'S NOT THE WORST OF IT.

MOVE

EVERYTHING

THE WORST IS THAT YOU'RE GOING TO HAVE TO COOK.

AND TO DO THAT, YOU'RE GOING TO NEED **TOOLS** TO COOK WITH.

SHIT, THE STRAINER!!

I FORGOT THE STRAINER!

YOU'LL SHOW UP HAGGARD, WANDERING LIKE A ZOMBIE, THROUGH THE AISLES OF IKEA© OR DARTY©.

LÜKSVIT

LÜKSVIT POT OR SASKAAD PAN?

PFF

LUGMA

YOU START TO DAYDREAM AND GET CARRIED AWAY BY YOUR THOUGHTS...

OOOH...

A SET OF EGG MOLDS...

WHAT IF I...

BECAUSE YOU DIDN'T KNOW THAT THERE'S A LIST...

DID I FORGET ANYTHING?

(MISSING THE PARING KNIFE SHE'S BEEN MEANING TO BUY FOR THREE MONTHS)

THE LIST OF...

A FEW USEFUL TOOLS FOR YOUR KITCHEN

NO MORE FORGETTING!

INK INK!

① TWO SHARP KNIVES ARE A GOOD START:

ONE SMALL

ONE BIG, WHILE YOU'RE AT IT

② A CUTTING BOARD MIGHT NOT SEEM LIKE MUCH BUT IS SUPER PRACTICAL:

LUXURY MODEL WITH A GROOVE TO KEEP ANY JUICES FROM LEAKING

③ A PEELER OR PARING KNIFE TO PEEL VEGETABLES:

MY PREFERRED MODEL

ANOTHER KIND

④ A GRATER FOR VARIOUS PEELED VEGETABLES:

THIS ONE IS PRACTICAL BUT ANNOYING TO CLEAN

⑤ A SAUCEPAN, BUT NOT ONE MADE OUT OF TIN--THEY STICK:

DECENT SIZE

SOLID HANDLE

⑥ A PAN OR A WOK, IF NOT BOTH:

LARGE DIAMETER, EASY TO HANDLE

DEEP, USEFUL FOR BIG DISHES

⑦ A LARGE POT FOR FAMILY STYLE DISHES:

GOOD HANDLES

MADE OF STAINLESS STEEL, LIGHT AND HANDY

A DURABLE CAST-IRON ONE THAT WILL LAST

⑧ A LARGE LID:

GROOVES TO FIT POTS OF ANY SIZE

NON-STICK COATING, USEFUL FOR FLIPPING OMELETS.

⑨ A MEASURING CUP, FOR BAKING:

IN GLASS, CLASSY BUT FRAGILE

IN PLASTIC, NOTHING TO FEAR (MINE IS TEN YEARS OLD)

⑩ A SCALE WHILE YOU'RE AT IT, ELECTRONIC OR MECHANICAL:

OLD SCHOOL

PRECISE MEASUREMENTS

⑪ A SALAD BOWL, FOR MIXING:

(NOTHING SPECIAL TO SAY HERE)

⑫ A WHISK OR ELECTRIC BEATER, IF NOT BOTH:

PRACTICAL FOR REMOVING LUMPS

BEST FOR WHIPPING EGG WHITES

⑬ A WOODEN SPOON AND A SPATULA:

FOR TOSSING

TO GRIP AND FLIP

⑭ A STRAINER, BUT NOT A PLASTIC ONE, THEY SUCK:

(SEE COMMENTS ON SALAD BOWL)

⑮ A CORKSCREW:

THE "DE GAULE" MODEL THAT RAISES ITS ARMS

I UNDERSTAND YOU!

VINEYARD MODEL, RUSTIC STYLE

⑯ A LADLE AND SKIMMER:

TO CLARIFY BROTHS

FOR SLURPING

⑰ A BAKING DISH:

ONE WITH HANDLES IS BEST

⑱ A PIE AND CAKE MOLD:

PYREX ONES ARE GREAT FOR PIZZA

SILICONE IS IDEAL

⑲ A CITRUS PRESS:

YOU CAN GET AN ELECTRIC ONE

...BUT A LITTLE EXERCISE NEVER HURT ANYONE

⑳ AN ELECTRIC MIXER:

SIMPLER MODEL

INDUSTRIAL FACTORY STYLE

㉑ A PAIR OF SCISSORS:

TO CUT PACKAGING AND STRINGS...

㉒ A GARLIC MILL:

THE HOLY GRAIL OF ALL CHEFS

㉓ A BRASS SAUCIER, NOT REQUIRED BUT VERY CLASSY:

IDEAL FOR BASIL SAUCES

㉔ A PESTLE:

STONE

WOOD

METAL

lon.

Pépé Roni's Good Advice: a whisk   n° 124

Don't confuse "a whip"   and a "whipper."   BECAUSE ANYONE CAN MAKE MISTAKES!

Whisk: A tool to whip, beat, or mix food items.

JOURNAL FROM BUDAPEST

DAY I

TRIP TO BUDAPEST

ON THE PLANE, I TRY NOT TO THINK ABOUT THE THOUSANDS OF FEET BETWEEN ME AND THE SOLID EARTH AND INSTEAD THINK ABOUT THE FORTUNE TO BE MADE IF AN AIRLINE COMPANY JUST HAD AN ITALIAN COFFEE MAKER ONBOARD.

EVERY TIME I TAKE THE PLANE, IT'S FOR THE LAST TIME.

NEXT TO US ON THE PLANE, A GUY TAKES MEDICINE.

I DRAW WHAT I'M LOOKING FORWARD TO IN BUDAPEST, GASTRONOMICALLY:

HUGE, DELICIOUS DESSERTS

GOULASH

REAL COFFEE

PAPRIKA EVERYWHERE

WORDS TO KNOW:
KÁVÉHÁZ = CAFÉ (THE PLACE)
ÉTTEREM = RESTAURANT
KÖSZÖNÖM = THANKS
HALLO = HELLO, HEY

HAJMINCZKY UT

KEUSSEUNEUM.

APPARENTLY, HUNGARIANS DON'T LIKE THE FRENCH.

FIRST MEAL IN HUNGARY AT THE GERLOCZY KÁVÉHÁZ, FIRST ENCOUNTER WITH LOCAL CUISINE:

OKAY, SO WHEN WE ORDER GOULASH WE GET A GOULASH *SOUP.*

WE HAVE TO ASK FOR PÖRKÖLT INSTEAD.

A TREE WITH HANGING BRANCHES AND POMPOMS OF FLOWERS

BREAKFAST (PRETTY GOOD, SPECIAL MENTION TO THE GOULASH SOUP) IN A SUNLIT PATIO BY A TREE. NANCY ORDERS SOME SORT OF CHICKEN STUFFED WITH CHEESE.

SERVICE

KYNLÖGÖTZÖ PLÖKTMENEKT WYGLÖNÖLÖT

KEUSSEUNEUM, DUDE

PLUGÖ, TRUKUL

IGEN, IGEN

15%.

WHEN YOU RECEIVE THE CHECK (USUALLY A NICE SURPRISE, AROUND 20 EUROS FOR TWO, EVEN WITH A GLASS OF WINE), YOU USUALLY HAVE TO LEAVE 10% TO 15% OF THE COST OF THE MEAL AS A TIP FOR THE SERVICE (TO BE PRECISE: IF THE SERVICE WAS GOOD).

WRÖLÖ TENEM

AND BECAUSE THE WAIT STAFF ARE GENERALLY VERY NICE, WE'RE USUALLY MORE THAN HAPPY TO PAY FOR THE SERVICE.

IF WE DID THE SAME THING IN PARIS, THE WAITERS WOULDN'T GET A DIME FOR THEIR SERVICE!

SERIOUSLY

(LIVED IN PARIS FOR 5 YEARS)

AT NIGHT, A FORGETTABLE DINNER AT THE DARSHAN, NEAR THE HOTEL. THE DECOR IS WEIRD--STUCK SOMEWHERE BETWEEN INDIA AND AFRICA. THEY SERVE EVERYTHING HERE: PIZZAS, GREEK SALADS, TANDOORI CHICKEN, AND STEAK TARTAR. SO, AS EXPECTED, EVERYTHING'S PRETTY AVERAGE.

DAY 2

A TRAP FOR THE SWEET-TOOTHED... WE SPEND SEVERAL HOURS INSIDE ONE OF THE TEMPLES OF HUNGARIAN PASTRIES...

A SORT OF PREAMBLE →

OH... WELL A REALLY SMALL SLICE THEN...

DESSERTS AREN'T REALLY MY THING, EXCEPT FOR MOM'S APPLE TARTS AND MOLTEN LAVA CAKE, OF COURSE...

IT LOOKS GOOD...

I JUST DON'T HAVE MUCH OF A SWEET TOOTH.

ANNO 1858 GERBEAUD BUDAPEST

PLENTY OF CAKES HERE!

THEY'LL DRIVE YOU CRAZY!

NANCY, I CAN'T...

YES, YOU CAN!

← CHOCOHOLIC

GERBEAUD, A SORT OF CATNIP FOR WOMEN

ISN'T THIS A LITTLE MUCH?

I DON'T REALLY LIKE SWEETS.

MONSTROUS BLACK FOREST SPONGE CAKE OVERFLOWING WITH CREAM, GENOISE, AND FLOATING CHOCOLATE

GLASSES OF WATER

CHOCOLATE PARFAIT VALRHONA (COME ON!!) WITH A CRUNCHY INTERIOR ↓

OMM NOMM NOM

RHAA, IT'S FINE, DON'T BE A WIMP.

CONTRARY TO MY EXPECTATIONS, THIS PASTRY CAFÉ IS A DELIGHT: THE DESSERTS ARE EXCELLENT (SPONGE CAKE) AND AS FULL OF CREAM AS THEY ARE LIGHT IN YOUR STOMACH, NO JOKE. DIDN'T EVEN MAKE ME SICK!

HINHIN! COFFEE! IN HUNGARY! HUHU!

SLRRRRP

WOW.

THAT'S GOOD.

REALLY GOOD.

NANSS TAKES A TRUE WOMAN'S COFFEE, A "MADEMOISELLE," WITH A PRONOUNCED TASTE OF CARAMEL TOPPED WITH A HEAPING PORTION OF WHIPPED CREAM. IT'S DELICIOUS.

YOU CAN TELL YOU'RE HAVING **GOOD COFFEE** BY THE FACT THAT IT'S ALWAYS SERVED WITH A GLASS OF WATER.

THE NIGHT

DINNER AT NÁROLY ETTEREM, NAROLY UT.

WE EAT DINNER IN A REALLY GREAT RESTAURANT, WITH A WONDERFUL BUDAPEST-STYLE DECOR: ARCHITECTURAL ARCHES, PAINTINGS, ORNAMENTS, AND A REDDISH-BROWN TINT.

YOU HAVE TO TAKE A PATH FROM THE STREET (UTCA) AND YOU ARRIVE IN A CHARMING INTERIOR HALL WHERE THE RESTAURANT IS.

THE DINNER STARTS OFF WELL WITH A DEER SOUP!! IT'S SERVED IN A BREAD BOWL-- A GREAT IDEA. THE SOUP IS FULL OF FLAVOR, WELL SPICED AND GAMEY (THOUGH I'VE NEVER HAD DEER BEFORE). IT'S ACCOMPANIED BY A GLASS OF TOKAJ WINE. I LIKE IT SO FAR.

THEN, I ORDER A ZANDER FILET WITH POTATOES...

BLACK BREAD FULL OF SOUP...

THE PROMISE

HUNGARIAN ZANDER STRAIGHT FROM THE BALATON!! ZANDER IS ALREADY A STAR AMONG FRESHWATER FISH, WITH A THIN FLESH, A GREAT SMELL, A TENDER TEXTURE, AND AN IVORY COLOR! ZANDER! FRESH ZANDER! FROM LAKE BALATON! HAND-FISHED!

THE REALITY

MY GOD

I'M SO DIS-APPOIN-TED

SO DIS-APPOINTED

THE ZANDER IS HERE, GLOOMY, TASTELESS, LYING DEAD IN THE MIDDLE OF THE PLATE WITH A MOUNTAIN OF WATERY, UNDERCOOKED POTATOES. IT'S PRACTICALLY CARDBOARD AND DOESN'T DESERVE TO BE CALLED FISH.

← NANCY ON HER SIDE

MMH, THIS IS DELICOUS! A CHICKEN FILET IN A POTATO CREPE. BUT I REALLY CAN'T HAVE A DESSERT.

challenge no1 :

Explain in English to a Hungarian the joke of Mr. and Mrs. "Gariansinmybathroomwhatcanido" who have a son*, in its entirety while in a bath:

(the main reason for this trip, joke wise)

* Gideon

challenge no 2:

Try to leave a restaurant without paying for the bill

IN ADDITION, **KOLEVES** (KAZINCZY UTCA) WAS REALLY GOOD. IT WAS IN THE OLD JEWISH GHETTO IN BUDAPEST. IT LOOKS LIKE A BISTRO AND ALL THE WAITERS WERE YOUNG.

I ORDER AN ARTICHOKE CREAM SOUP AND SOME PINK DUCK BREAST WITH AN APPLE AND POTATO PUREE.

THERE ARE LAMPS MADE FROM IKEA GRATERS AND THESE REALLY NICE DRAWINGS AND PAINTINGS EVERYWHERE. VERY COOL!

AND WHAT DO I GET?
WELL, *EXACTLY* WHAT I ORDERED. IT'S DELICIOUS AND LOOKS GREAT, *EXCEPT* THAT I HADN'T ENVISIONED IT BEING QUITE SO...

WHEN WE PAY WITH A CREDIT CARD IN THE RESTAURANTS HERE, YOU CAN READ THIS AT THE BOTTOM OF YOUR RECEIPT:

ZICHY

THE HARDEST THING AFTER THAT KIND OF BREAKFAST IS THAT YOU STILL HAVE TO EAT THROUGHOUT THE DAY.

AMERICAN EMBASSY

NO SKETCHES

NO PHOTO

WELL, EVENTUALLY WE ARRIVE AT **RUSZWURM**

...ANOTHER GREAT LITTLE BAKERY HERE

IT'S FINE, I HAD FRUIT THIS MORNING!

BUT SO DID I!

IN BUDAPEST, YOU EAT AND YOU GET FAT, NO WAY AROUND IT.

"HUNGARIAN PROVERB"

IF GERBEAUD WAS A PARADISE FOR WOMEN, RUSZWURM IS THE ANTECHAMBER.

THE ALL-IMPORTANT GLASS OF WATER

CHOCOLATE MONSTROSITY WITH HAZELNUT CREAM

DELICIOUS APPLE STRUDEL, DON'T MISS IT IF YOU COME TO BUDAPEST.

ICED COFFEE, CHOCOLATE WITH VANILLA CREAM

I HAVE TO ADMIT THAT THIS GIRL'S COFFEE IS VERY GOOD, BUT WITH ALL THESE SWEETS AND HANDBAGS...

YOU'D THINK WE WERE AT JENNYFER DURING A SALE.

RUSZWURM

BURP

NORMAL, THAT IS TO SAY, EXQUISITE, COFFEE

WITH EXTRA CREAM

AND THEN WE EAT AT

MOST!*

ZICHY JENŐ UTCA, 17

* NOW

A BISTRO WITH MISMATCHED TABLES AND CHAIRS:

A BISTRO WITH MEN WHO SMOKE WHILE THEY EAT IN FRONT OF THEIR LAPTOPS:

CANDLESTICK BOTTLE

A BISTRO WITH WAITRESSES AND A TAPESTRY OF BOOKS. VERY FEW TOURISTS IF ANY.

IT'S NOT NECESSARILY HUNGARIAN FOOD, BUT IT'S SIMPLE AND GOOD. THE CHEF'S NAME IS GURUNG. HE MAKES INDONESIAN DISHES AMONG OTHERS.

A BUSY, HIP, MODERN BISTRO, WITH USB PORTS AND A STAGE:

ARCHED CEILING

MISMATCHED BAR

STAGE

THE ROOM

STEAMED PORK BALLS

YOU CAN'T TELL, BUT A GLASS OF WINE HERE IS HUGE. HUGE!

SPINACH AND RICOTTA GNOCCHI.

WE ORDER THE SOUP OF THE DAY, BUT THE WAITRESS SPOILS THE MYSTERY.

HÉ HO! IT'S OKAY WE ARE NOT IN SUGAR HEIN

WHITE BEANS

SHE'S THINKING WE ARE FUCKING TOURISTS

WELL, THEIR SOUP ISN'T VERY INTERESTING TO DRAW, BUT IT'S DELICIOUS.

NANSS GETS A RECOMMENDATION FOR A DELICIOUS WHITE WINE:

"IRSAI OLIVÉR NYAKAS" FRESH, FRUITY, AND TASTES LIKE WHITE RAISINS. A MUST TRY!!

DAY 5

I'LL WARN YOU RIGHT NOW, IT'S A DARK DAY FOR GASTRONOMY.

ON THIS DAY, MY STOMACH EXPERIENCED ITS OWN APOCALYPSE.

WHAT? ? HUH?

IT DIDN'T START THAT WAY, THOUGH...

NAGY VASARCSARNOK
(CENTRAL MARKET, NA'MHA'Z, KÖRÜT, 1-3)

CAN YOU GET UP NOW?

WOOOAH IT'S SO COOL!

THOUSANDS OF SQUARE FEET ON TWO FLOORS MADE OF IRON AND GLASS, ENTIRELY DEDICATED TO FOOD!! IT REMINDS ME OF THE ENORMOUS MARKET IN BARCELONA (SAINT JOSEPH'S).

CHARCUTERIE, SPICES, VEGETABLES. ALL LIVING TOGETHER IN PACKED STALLS. THERE'S A WHOLE ETIQUETTE TO IT IN HUNGARY THAT I HAVE NO CLUE ABOUT, BUT I DON'T MIND.

ON THE UPPER FLOOR, WE EAT SIDE BY SIDE WITH HUNGARIANS AND OTHER TOURISTS. PEOPLE SMOKE. THE FOOD IS FATTY AND RICH. IT'S BEAUTIFUL.

GUIGUI AT THE EXIT OF THE MARKET IN BUDAPEST WITH SOME SALAMI, RADISHES, TOKAJ, AND SPICES. (A FEW HOURS BEFORE THE ORDEAL)

ON OUR PLATES, MEATBALLS MADE WITH SOME SORT OF UNKNOWN MEAT, RICE SPICED WITH PAPRIKA, AND MYSTERY CROQUETTES. I WOULDN'T SAY IT WAS GOOD, I WOULD SAY IT WAS FATTY AND THAT IT LACKED TASTE.

"KRÚJMÜT VLAPÖ PICK SKIYSCNYÉLT"*

* PICK, SIMPLY THE BEST

BUT NAN, I DIDN'T SAY ANYTHING IN HUNGARIAN, I JUST WROTE SOME NONSENSE THAT WOULD SOUND HUNGARIAN...

AND I DON'T EVEN KNOW VLAPÖ, HOW COULD I HAVE TOLD HIM TO GO SHOVE A SALAMI UP HIS ASS?

THE GOOD TIMES CONTINUED WELL INTO

CENTRAL KÁVÉHÁZ

CRAZY DECOR ALL AROUND, VERY 19TH CENTURY

SOME REAL COFFEE

BUT REALLY COMPLICATED TO DRAW, WITH ITS BIZARRE PERSPECTIVE

WE HAD AN ESPRESSO PEPPERINO (COFFEE, CHOCOLATE AND PEPPER-- KILLER!) AND A KAPUCINER, WHICH ACTUALLY MADE ME APPRECIATE CAPUCCINO AS A COFFEE.

NO... THE HORROR OF MY CULINARY VIETNAM TRULY STARTED WITH...

HORGASZTANYA*

IT STARTS LIKE ORGASM, BUT IT FINISHES LIKE TENIA*

*TAPEWORM

* THE FISHERMAN'S FARM, FÖ UTCA 27

THINGS STARTED OUT WELL, AT FIRST:

DEAL

HIGHLY RECOMMENDED BY THE PEOPLE HERE, AND MY GUIDE SAYS THAT THE FISH SCALE SOUP IS DELICIOUS!

EFFECTIVELY:

WE ORDER A CATFISH SOUP AND IT'S DELICIOUS. IT'S NOT TOO FILTERED SO IT'S KIND OF LIKE A BOUILLABAISSE, AND THERE ARE LARGE PIECES OF FISH INSIDE!

THE RESTAURANT'S DECOR IS A LITTLE KITSCH, IT'S FUNNY... THERE ARE A BUNCH OF FISHING TOOLS, OPTICAL ILLUSIONS, NETTING...

DID YOU SEE THE BOAT ON THE CEILING?

SEEMS LIKE A POPULAR PLACE.

BUT EVERYTHING TOOK A TURN FOR THE WORSE WHEN WE DECIDED TO:

OOOOH THERE'S A DISH WITH PERCH, ZANDER, CARP, AND CATFISH!

LIVING A DREAM

FOR TWO... CAN WE TRY IT?

HAVE SOME GNOCCHI* WITH IT.

EEEH! I'M GOING TO DIE!!!

* IN HUNGARY, GNOCCHI ARE SPÄTZLE

THE PROMISE

THE BEST FRESHWATER FISH ALL TOGETHER IN A SINGLE DISH! FRESHLY FISHED FROM LAKE BALATON! THE DREAM OF EVERY AMATEUR FISH-LOVER COME TRUE, SERVED ON A SILVER PLATTER!

THE REALITY

BREADED

BREADED

MOUNTAIN OF COLD SPÄTZLE

SAME

TUBE OF TARTAR SAUCE

CAMERA OF THE INSIDE OF MY STOMACH:

FRRH

I'M MELTING!

RETREAT! RETREAT!

SO... HOW SHOULD I PUT THIS... WELL, IF YOU PULLED OFF THE SIDE OF A HIGHWAY AND ORDERED FOUR PLATES OF BREADED FISH THAT YOU THEN DROWNED IN OIL AND RANDOMLY DUSTED WITH SUGAR (SERIOUSLY!), AND THEN ON THE SIDE YOU TOOK A POT OF COLD, UNSALTED SPÄTZLE, YOU'D GET APPROXIMATELY THE SAME END RESULT.

IT WASN'T GOOD. AT ALL. IT WAS SO BAD THAT IT TOOK AWAY MY DESIRE TO LIVE. IT KILLS ME TO HAVE FISH COOKED THAT WAY. I LEFT THREE-QUARTERS OF IT ON THE PLATE.

LATER...

(BEHIND US, THE DANUBE ALL LIT UP)

EVEN LATER...

I DON'T THINK THERE'S ANYTHING WORSE THAN BEING DISAPPOINTED BY A RESTAURANT. ACTUALLY, MAYBE MESSING UP A DINNER YOU COOK FOR YOUR GUESTS. BUT THAT'S IT.

57TH DAY: IT'S BEEN ALMOST TWO MONTHS SINCE I LANDED IN HUNGARY. THE ELEMENTS HAVE BEEN PARTICULARLY ACTIVE THESE LAST FEW WEEKS AND I'VE BEEN LOSING MY MEMORY EVER SINCE I ATE A PARTICULAR BITTER DISH OF BREADED FISH... THE CLIMATE AND FOOD GOT THE BEST OF MY BELOVED, I BURIED HER LAST WEEK. I WALK DEEPER INTO THE HUNGARIAN JUNGLE, ON THE HUNT FOR PÖRKÖLT, DRINKING FROM THE PUDDLES OF THE TOKAJ, BUT STILL ALIVE.

I NOTICED THAT THE HUNGARIANS WEAR A SORT OF GLASS CAGE AROUND THEIR HEADS, WHICH MAKES IT IMPOSSIBLE FOR THEM TO COMMUNICATE.

FORTUNATELY, I MANAGED TO FIND A HAMMER TO BREAK THE GLASS, AND UNDERNEATH DISCOVERED A VERY CHARMING PEOPLE.

I USE THIS TECHNIQUE QUITE OFTEN, MOST NOTABLY IN A SMALL SHOP WHERE I BOUGHT SOME MEDICINE FOR INDIGESTION.

HOLLO MUHELY

VIKTOVICS MIHA'LY UTCA, 12. CENTRAL PEST

A REALLY, REALLY COOL, UNDERAPPRECIATED, ARTISANAL STORE WHERE I MET LÁSZLÓ HOLLÓ, A GUY WHO PAINTS EGGS AND OTHER OBJECTS WITH A HUNGARIAN MOTIF. HE EVEN HAS A LITTLE WORKSHOP CONNECTED TO HIS SHOP. WE SPOKE IN A SORT OF BROKEN ENGLISH, ABOUT HOW HARD IT IS TO LIVE AN ARTISTIC LIFE, AND INDULGED IN A LITTLE NOSTALGIA FOR A TIME THAT WAS LESS... CAPITALIST.

AT THE HOTEL.

HiAiHi

SHARKOZY

WHEN ARE YOU GOING TO GO TO SLEEP?

HUH! WHAT?

NO, NO. I'M WORKING ON MY JOURNAL RIGHT NOW.

SO, UH... WHERE WERE WE...

DAY 6

AHA, TODAY'S THE DAY. TODAY, WE'RE BACK TO FOOD!

137 LBS

AT THE **KOR** CAFÉ

(WHAT ARE YOU COOKING UP NOW?)

GAL TIBOR EGRI BIKAVÉR (A RED BLEND FROM THE EGER REGION OF HUNGARY, MADE WITH KÉKFRANKOS, MERLOT, AND CABERNET FRANC GRAPES.)

BÁRÁNYPÖRKÖLT (LAMB STEW)

VÖRÖS BÉLSZÍN PÖRKÖLT (RED BEEF TENDERLOIN STEW)

WE EAT REALLY WELL, IN THIS SORT OF CAFE-BISTRO WHERE THE WAITERS WEAR THESE LARGE WHITE APRONS.

THE PORTIONS ARE SO HUGE IN HUNGARY THAT YOU QUICKLY LOSE SIGHT OF THE TYPICAL APPETIZER-ENTREE-DESSERT TRILOGY.

KEUSSEUNEEUM!

DESPITE THAT, NANCY GETS CLEVER AND ORDERS:

A CHEESE PLATTER?

THEY DON'T BRING YOU THE WHOLE DAMN PLATTER TO EAT IN FRANCE!!

ALL FRENCH CHEESES, DELICIOUS AND ON POINT

I TOLD YOU, I'M NOT HAVING ANY.

AND I, PRINCE THAT I AM, DECIDE TO HELP HER A BIT BY HAVING A LITTLE BIT OF THE FRESH GOAT CHEESE.

OH SHIT. IT'S BUTTER!

AND THEN AT KÁRPÁTIA

FERENCIEK TERE 7-8

JUST AS BAD, WITH CRAZY DECOR, AND THE MUSICIANS AND WAITERS WORKING IN SYNC TO SERVE AND REMOVE DISHES IN RHYTHM WITH THE MUSIC.

JUST KIDDING... THE KÁRPÁTIA IS GOOD, LIGHT, AND MIXES TRADITIONAL AND MODERN CUISINE. IF YOU'RE IN BUDAPEST, CHECK IT OUT. IT'S A **LITTLE** MORE EXPENSIVE THAN OTHER PLACES, BUT IT'S WORTH THE DETOUR.

DAY 7 IN OTHER WORDS, THE SEVENTH DAY. WHEN WE REFLECT ON THE WORK WE'VE DONE AND SEE THAT IT WAS GOOD...

THAT'S WHAT I HAVE TO SAY ABOUT IT.

FINALLY, WHAT'S A **PÖRKÖLT?**

A week of study.

(1) GOOD, SIMPLE INGREDIENTS

VEAL SHOULDER IN CUBES

ONIONS

PEPPERS

SOFT AND SHARP PAPRIKA

SALT

PEPPER

TOMATOES

BAY LEAVES

VEAL STOCK OR WATER

OIL

(2) MINCE THE ONIONS AND SWEAT THEM WITH OIL IN A PAN UNTIL THEY BECOME TRANSLUCENT.

TSCHHH

(3) THEN LOWER THE HEAT TO THE MINIMUM AND ADD ALL THE VEAL AND SHARP PAPRIKA, UNTIL THE MEAT TAKES COLOR...

IF YOU BURN THE PAPRIKA, IT'LL BECOME BITTER.

BAY LEAF

SO SLOWLY.

THE MORE PAPRIKA YOU ADD, THE THICKER YOUR SAUCE WILL BE.

(4) AND THEN COVER IT ALL WITH THE STOCK, ADD A LITTLE SALT AND PEPPER, AND LET IT SIMMER FOR AN HOUR ON A LOW FIRE.

THE MEAT HAS TO COOK IN THE STOCK FOR THE SAUCE TO THICKEN.

FLOP FLOP FLOP

(5) ADD THE DICED TOMATOES, THE PEPPERS IN LARGE PIECES, AND THEN LET IT SIMMER FOR ANOTHER HOUR WHILE MAKING SURE THERE'S ENOUGH STOCK THAT NOTHING STICKS TOGETHER.

(6) SERVE IT UP NICE AND HOT, SEASON WITH A LITTLE BIT OF SOFT PAPRIKA, WITH SOME BOILED OR BAKED POTATOES.

WELL, THAT'S IT. A NICE, FILLING DISH. NOTHING PARTICULARLY AMAZING. SIMPLE AND DELICIOUS. BUT IT'S NOTHING TO ROLL ON THE FLOOR OVER.

JADED AFTER 10,000 PÖRKÖLTS.

AND THEN AT THE

BORSSÓ
BISTRO
(KIRALYIPAL UTCA, 14)

WE'RE ROLLING ON THE FLOOR!

IT'S SO GOOD!

GROOO

FORGOT THAT HE HAS TO TAKE A PLANE IN A FEW HOURS.

I THINK IT'S THE BEST RESTAURANT I ATE AT HERE... HUNGARIAN CUISINE REINVENTED, A DECONSTRUCTED PÖRKÖLT, A BURST GOULASH. WELL, IT WAS INCREDIBLE.

GREAT PRESENTATION, DELICIOUS FLAVORS

LAMB PÖRKÖLT WITH CREPES

KIRALY PAUL IXERKÁBORUM LIKE THE ALBIS WINES

GÜJNER ÖROGAROK NADARKA THAT TASTES LIKE LICORICE AND PEPPER

VEAL MEDALLION AND VEGETABLE CROQUETTES

AFTER EVERYTHING ELSE, IT'S TIME FOR DESSERT:

DARK CHOCOLATE VOLCANO CAKE

SPONGE CAKE

WITH A LOT OF CREAM

EPILOGUE

WE TAKE THE PLANE HOME IN THE AFTERNOON. A CLOUDY SKY. WE'RE GOING TO DIE. THE STEWARDESS IS SMILING WEIRDLY. EVERY TIME THE PLANE SHAKES IS MY LAST TIME. FEELING LIKE WE'RE GOING TO CRASH LIKE LOST...

PLANE THAT'S FLOWN A THOUSAND TIMES

2000 MILES FROM HERE, A VOLCANO ERUPTED, PARALYZING ALL AIR TRAFFIC IN EUROPE FOR A WEEK... TOO BAD, I COULD'VE EASILY SPENT A FEW EXTRA DAYS HERE, AND WE COULD'VE TAKEN THE TRAIN INSTEAD.

Pépé Roni's Good Advice: browning — n° 103

Don't confuse "watching over your flock"

and "watching over your work."

BECAUSE ANYONE CAN MAKE MISTAKES!

Browning: to bring color to an ingredient in a heated fat, generally before further cooking.

Summer

THE TOMATOES
THAT I'VE TASTED

FROM MEMORY!

PINEAPPLE

A YELLOW TOMATO. BESIDES ITS COLOR, WHICH IS THE REASON I BOUGHT IT IN THE FIRST PLACE, I HAVE NO OTHER MEMORABLE THINGS TO SHARE ABOUT THIS FRUIT.

CHERRY

THE BEST APPETIZER TOMATO. PRETTY ACIDIC. CURIOUSLY, IT'S DELICIOUS REGARDLESS OF WHETHER YOU GET IT FROM A SUPERMARKET OR GROW THEM YOURSELF.

BEEFSTEAK

I'VE ALWAYS BEEN DISAPPOINTED BY THESE MOSTLY TASTELESS TOMATOES WHEN I'VE BOUGHT THEM. IF YOU GET THEM FROM A GARDEN, THOUGH, THEY'RE KILLER!

DIPLOM F1

THE FIRST TOMATO I GREW AND HARVESTED, SO IT'S OBVIOUSLY A TOMATO I LOOK BACK UPON FONDLY.

GRAPE

OFTEN BOUGHT IN SUPERMARKETS. I FIND THESE REALLY TASTE LIKE TOMATOES. THOUGH CURRENTLY PRETTY POPULAR, I'VE FOUND THEIR QUALITY TO BE DECREASING.

KUMATO

A TOMATO THAT'S BROWN AND PRETTY EXPENSIVE, WHICH MADE ME REALLY WANT TO TRY IT AT THE TIME. IN THE END, IT'S NO BETTER THAN A GRAPE TOMATO, THIS REALLY ISN'T "THE" TOMATO.

MARMANDE TOMATO

REALLY EASY TO GROW. THESE FRUITS ARE LARGE AND SMELL GREAT. THEY'RE PERFECT FOR MAKING BAKED TOMATOES.

MONTFAVET

I BARELY REMEMBER THIS ONE, BUT I'M SURE I'VE HAD IT BEFORE.

BLACK KRIM

REALLY DELICIOUS GARDEN TOMATO, SOFT, WITH A FULL FLESH.

PLUM

I RECENTLY DISCOVERED THIS TOMATO IN SALADS. IT'S GREAT FOR SAUCES AND HAS A LIGHT TASTE OF PEPPER.

ROMA

ANOTHER SAUCE TOMATO WITH A LOT OF PULP. A VERY ITALIAN STYLE, LIKE OUT OF A BARILLA®.

ROSE DE BERNE

A TOMATO SO PINK YOU WONDER IF IT'S EVER GOING TO RIPEN. IT'S NAME MAKES IT SOUND LIKE SOMETHING OUT OF A BARBARA CARTLAND NOVEL. SOFT AND SWEET.

ROUND

AS DELICIOUS TO TASTE AS IT WAS FUN TO DRAW... THAT IS TO SAY, NOT VERY. I ONLY KNOW THEM FROM SUPERMARKETS AND, FOR A LONG TIME, THOUGHT I DIDN'T LIKE TOMATOES BECAUSE OF THEM.

SAINT-PIERRE

A GOOD, BIG TOMATO. VERY PLUMP AND REWARDING TO GROW IN YOUR OWN HERB GARDEN.

SARDINIA

THE BEST TOMATO I'VE EVER HAD! VERY FIRM WITH AN ACIDIC TASTE. YOU SHOULD EAT IT WHEN IT'S STILL GREEN. YOU CAN FIND THEM IN SUPERMARKETS IN SWITZERLAND. THEY'RE EXPENSIVE, BUT WORTH EVERY PENNY. THEY'RE BEST TO HAVE IN A SALAD.

YELLOW PEAR

ANOTHER APPETIZER TOMATO, RELATIVELY SWEET, AND GREAT FOR DECORATING YOUR DISHES WITH A LITTLE COLOR.

leon.

I LOVE FISH.

FISH FOR APPETIZERS

SO CUTE!

Jols Fritter

FRIED, GRILLED, EN PAPILLOTE, RAW, OR COOKED IN A COURT BOUILLON...

OOOH... LITTLE OCTOPUSES

HIHI

Octopus Salad

With parsley and garlic

IF I COULD I WOULD EAT ALL THE FISH IN THE WORLD.

A COMBER!

RAINBOW WRASSE!

A GRAY WRASSE!

PORGY!

FISH SOUP
with rouille

I REMEMBER WHEN I SAW THE MOVIE OCEANS, I WAS HUNGRY THE ENTIRE TIME.

A CAPELIN!

SCORPION FISH!

A WEE-VER...

Bouillabaise

AND I WOULDN'T HESITATE TO CHOOSE GRILLED SEABASS OVER BEEF RIBS.

POISSONNER

RHÂÂÂÂARGL

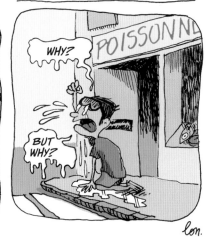

HELLO!

WHAT?

YOU'RE CRAZY! OF COURSE MY FISH IS FRESH! THEY CAME THIS MORNING, RUNGIS!

WHY?

BUT WHY?

lon.

YOU MIGHT HAVE NOTICED IT IN RESTAURANTS, CAFES, OR EVEN TEA HOUSES...

DISTINGUISHED PEOPLE ALWAYS KEEP THEIR PINKIES RAISED.

WELL, IT MIGHT LOOK NICE, BUT IT'S NOT PART OF ANY SORT OF ELEGANT TRADITION! QUITE THE OPPOSITE IN FACT!

OH? IS THAT SO?

LET US REWIND A BIT THROUGH HISTORY... TO A TIME WHEN SITTING AT THE TABLE WAS AN ADVENTURE UNTO ITSELF.

THE FIRST RULE OF ELEGANCE WAS TO EAT CLEANLY AND TO KEEP YOUR PINKY RAISED:

BURRRP

THE SECOND RULE OF ELEGANCE WAS TO AVOID GETTING FOOD ALL OVER YOURSELF, KEEPING YOUR PINKY IN THE AIR.

MIOM GLUP SLURP BRÖT

THE THIRD RULE... WELL, CAN WE REALLY STILL TALK ABOUT ELEGANCE AT THIS POINT? HOPEFULLY YOU HAVEN'T MISSED THAT THIS PIG...

CHOMPS! BOUFFE

HAS KEPT HIS PINKY IN THE AIR!

HUHU! HU!

BUT WHY?

WELL... WHEN YOU EAT A NICE TURKEY LEG WITH YOUR HANDS, AND THEY GET COVERED IN FAT...

BUT... I... I NEVER... I...

HAVE YOU EVER TRIED TO SERVE YOURSELF SOME SALT, OR MUSTARD, OR SPICES?

THAT'S WHY HAVING YOUR PINKY DRY BECAME A COMMON PRACTICE!

AND IT'S GREAT FOR SCRATCHING OUR EAR, TOO! TIME FOR A LITTLE PAPRIKA WOW, I'M A MESS!

SO INSTEAD OF ADOPTING THESE BOORISH MANNERS, WHY NOT LET YOURSELF GO A LITTLE...

CHAARLES!! SUGAR FOR TABLE 12!

MA'AM

THAT SAID, BEWARE OF IMITATIONS.

SOME "PEOPLE" DON'T KEEP THEIR PINKY RAISED OUT OF TRADITION...

CH-CHARLES. WHY... WHY ARE YOU LOOKING AT ME LIKE THAT?

CHARLES?

WHEN IT STARTS TO GET HOT, THE INK THICKENS, THE PIECES OF PAPER STICK TO MY FOREARMS, AND I FEEL A STRANGE SENSATION:

I'M NOT VERY HUNGRY.

THE ONLY THING I CRAVE IN THOSE MOMENTS IS A DELICIOUS, FRESH TOMATO SALAD.

PFF...

SAUSAGES, EGGS...

LAME

LEEKS

TORTELLINI

BROCCOLI

WELP

RACLETTE...

BLEGH

THE PROBLEM IS THAT IT'S HARD TO BUY GOOD TOMATOES. EVEN AT THE FARMER'S MARKET. EVEN IF THEY'RE ORGANIC.

APPARENTLY IT'S BECAUSE THEY DON'T GROW THEM IN THE OPEN GROUND ANYMORE.

8 0C

AND IF YOU GROW THEM IN YOUR GARDENS, AT LEAST WHERE I LIVE, THE BEGINNING OF SUMMER IS STILL FAR TOO EARLY FOR THEM.

FORTUNATELY (NATURE IS WELL DESIGNED), WE CAN FIND...

devotion

humility

worship

prostration

THE SARDINIAN TOMATO

IMAGINE... SARDINIA. THE BLACK LAND, THE SPARKLING SEA, AND THE "CAMONE" TOMATOES AS FAR AS YOU CAN SEE...

KSS-KSS
KSS-KSS KSS
KSS-KSS KSS-KSS
KSS-KSS
KSS-KSS
KSS-KSS
KSS

A CRISP SKIN, AN ACIDIC TASTE, A BEAUTIFUL GREEN AND RED SKIN... IT'S "THE TOMA

EXCUSE ME.

SARDINIANS?

HOW DARE YOU! SARDINIANS! AS THE MINISTER OF FRENCH PRODUCTS, I CAN'T ALLOW YOU--

OH, IT'S FINE.

I'M THE MINISTER OF TRUCKS AND THIS IS ALL FINE BY ME.

?

TRUCKS! IS THAT WHAT WE'VE COME TO? I'M THE MINISTER OF THE ENVIRONMENT AND PLASTICS, AND I'D LIKE TO REMIND YOU THAT SOON THERE WILL BE NO--

PFF

PFF

YES, SO, ANYWAY. I'M COMPLETELY CRAZY ABOUT THIS TOMATO (IT'S PRETTY EXPENSIVE, BUT TOTALLY WORTH THE PRICE) IN SALADS! SINCE IT MATURES BETWEEN DECEMBER AND JUNE, IT'S IDEAL FOR THE EARLY SUMMER!

FOR MY ABSOLUTE FAVORITE SALAD, YOU'LL NEED:

SARDINIAN "CAMONE" TOMATOES

SALT FROM GUERANDE

5-PEPPER BLEND

A TON OF FLAT-LEAF PARSLEY OR BASIL

WHITE BALSAMIC VINEGAR

A DELICIOUS OLIVE OIL

I START BY CUTTING MY TOMATOES, FOLLOWING THE SAME PROCESS I ALWAYS DO.

I KNOW IT'S A BIT SILLY.

HEY! DID HE EVEN HEAR US?

I DON'T THINK SO. NO.

BUT IT SAVES TIME.

I REMEMBER THAT IT WAS COOL, AT FIRST.

YEAH... EVERYONE WANTED THE SAME CUT!

IT WAS IN STYLE!

AND THEN IT ALL WENT TO HELL.

I MEAN, SERIOUSLY, WE'D RATHER BE JULIENNED!

THIS IS THE WORST!

YEAH! WHEN IT WAS JUST ONE OF US, IT WAS OKAY...

BUT WHEN THERE'S SO MANY OF US, IT STARTS TO CAUSE PROBLEMS.

YEAH

I DON'T KNOW ABOUT YOU, BUT WHEN I HAVE A NEW COOKING GADGET, I GET THIS GREAT FEELING!

POMPOLOM ♪♪ IT'S NOT UNUSUAL TO BE LOVED BY ANYONE ♪♪

WELL, UH...

IT'S STARTING TO BE A LITTLE MUCH...

CAN'T WE JUST GET ROASTED, LIKE WE USED TO?

IT'S CALLED A *SPIRELLI©.* I SAW IT ONLINE...

GOOGLE STAR WARS KENNER GADGET SEARCH DARTH VADER IN STAINLESS STEEL SEARCH BABY ANIMAL VIDEOS SEARCH COOKING POTS

NAAAN...

SPIRELLI©... HMM...

Quick to make...

EXPRESS ZUCCHINI SALAD

Quick to eat!

YOU'LL NEED:

YOUNG ZUCCHINI   LEMON

SALT   PEPPER   OLIVE OIL   BALSAMIC VINEGAR

HERBS YOU LIKE →

(1) ONCE YOU'VE PEELED THE **YOUNG** ZUCCHINI AND CUT OFF THE EDGES:

GRATE THEM FINELY INTO VERMICELLI.

(2) YOU PRESS THE LEMON:

AND THEN YOU SOAK THE GRATED ZUCCHINI WITH THE LEMON JUICE, ADDING A GOOD DRIZZLE OF OLIVE OIL, A DASH OF BALSAMIC VINEGAR, AND SALT AND PEPPER.

(3) IF YOU WANT, YOU CAN ADD SOME OTHER HERBS, LIKE:

CORIANDER   PARSLEY   CHIVES   MINT

EAT IT RIGHT AWAY, OR ELSE THE ZUCCHINI WILL LET OFF SOME WATER AND IT WON'T BE AS GOOD.

IT'S GREAT FOR LUNCH IN THE SUMMER WHEN YOU DON'T HAVE MUCH TIME!

OF COURSE, IF YOU HAVE A SPIRELLI©, IT'S THAT MUCH EASIER!

HEHE!

lon.

Pépé Roni's Good Advice: Blued Trout   nº 039

Don't confuse a "blue" trout

?

and a "blued" trout.

BECAUSE ANYONE CAN MAKE MISTAKES!

Blued trout (truite au bleu): a way of cooking that involves plunging the fish rigorously while fresh so that it retains all of its mucus and then cooking it in a vinegar court-bouillon, which turns the fish blue.

WHEN IT'S THIS HOT, I ALREADY DON'T WANT TO DRAW, BUT WHAT REALLY KILLS ME IS...

I'M NOT THAT HUNGRY.

THE ONLY THING I CRAVE IN THESE MOMENTS IS...

PFF...

DARN, NOTHING TO EAT.

FONDUE... UGH!

NUL

NOTH- ING AT ALL!

THE ONLY THING, I--

WELL YES, YOU THERE...

THERE'S WHAT?

GO ON, SAY IT.

WHAT?

SARDINIAN TOMATOES?

WHAT?

I ALREADY TALKED ABOUT IT?

NO, BUT OF COURSE I...

HEH, WAIT AND SEE!

YOU THINK I DON'T KNOW WHAT I'VE ALREADY DRAWN!

ALL THESE EXTRAVA- GANT BACKGROUNDS...

AND EXPLANATIONS OF FOOD...

I MADE ALL OF THIS.

SO, NO, I'M NOT TALKING ABOUT THOSE TOMATOES AGAIN.

AND, YES, I KNOW I'M REUSING THE SAME PANELS.

BUT WITH THIS HEAT, I REALLY DON'T WANT TO DRAW.

SO, WHERE WAS I AGAIN?

RIGHT.

WELL:

THE ONLY THING I WANT WHEN IT'S THIS HOT, IS WHAT I'LL CALL...

FRANCINE'S DRINK

JUST BECAUSE I GOT THE RECIPE FROM FRANCINE.

IT'S REALLY EASY:

FIRST YOU HAVE TO MAKE A TILIA INFUSION.

I KNOW, THE BACK- GROUNDS...

THEY'RE THE WORST TO DRAW WHEN IT'S HOT.

FOR A ONE-LITER BOTTLE, YOU'LL NEED: ABOUT ONE LITER OF WATER AND A GOOD ARMFUL OF TILIA. PLUS IT'S IN SEASON IN THE SUMMER:

INFUSE IT IN HOT WATER FOR ABOUT 10 MINUTES, THEN REMOVE THE TILIA WITH A SKIMMER AND LET IT COOL.

THEN, PRESS THE LEMON AND ADD IT TO THE BOTTLE.

AND THEN, ADD THE INFUSION.

PERSONALLY, I LIKE IT WITH VERY LITTLE SUGAR, SO I ONLY ADD A LITTLE BIT OF LIQUID CANE SUGAR.

CANE SUGAR

INFUSION

LEMON

PURE JOY.

ESPECIALLY WHEN IT'S NICE AND COLD.

MINISTER OF LAZINESS AND BORDER CONTROL, WHAT IS THIS COMIC?

AUGUST SUCKS.

lon.

YOU'RE SWISS... BUT IT'S NOT YOUR FAULT.

HEY!

WHAT ARE YOU TRYING TO SAY?

THE MUSTACHE, ON THE OTHER HAND, IS.

FOR A LONG TIME, YOU WENT TO BED AT A REASONABLE HOUR. PERHAPS THAT WOULD MAKE A GOOD COMIC BOOK, BUT THAT'S BESIDE THE POINT...

NO... WHAT WE CARE ABOUT HERE IS THAT AS A SWISS PERSON, YOU KNOW ONE OF THE COOLEST SUPERMARKETS IN THE WORLD.

FAIR ENOUGH.

COOP

AT THE *COOP,* YOU'VE BOUGHT

CUORI DI CARCIOFINI

IT'S WORTH SAYING THAT IT'S THE COOLEST PRODUCT IN THE COOLEST SUPERMARKET IN THE ENTIRE WORLD.

FOR A LONG TIME, YOU JUSTIFIED THE PURCHASE BY EXPLAINING:

WE--WE CAN ALWAYS USE IT IN CASE OF A NUCLEAR--

FINE.

SHEESH!

AND FOR A LONG TIME, YOU ATE THAT VERY SAME BOX OF ARTICHOKE HEARTS WITH OLIVE OIL.

OH COME ON! THAT'S NOT OKAY!

EEK!

BUT, FOR A LONG TIME, YOU'VE ALSO MADE THE SAME MISTAKE.

HEY GOD, HOW ARE YOU?

ACTUALLY, I AM MAKING SURE TO USE THE LEFTOVER OLIVE OIL TO MAKE SALAD SAUCES!

NO, ANOTHER ERROR.

NO, IT'S FINE... I'M SORTING THE GLASS.

AND THE PAPER FROM THE STICKER.

THERE IT IS. THE PAPER. FOR A LONG TIME YOU THREW AWAY THE STICKER OF THE *CUORI DI CARCIOFINI.*

WAIT, WHAT?

I'M NOT SUPPOSED TO?

IT'S WRONG?

HAHA! THE STICKER, MY FRIEND, IS THE KEY! YOU'VE NEVER THOUGHT TO LOOK *ON THE OTHER SIDE* OF THE STICKER!

THE STICK...

OH MY! OH MY!

A RECIPE!

A RECIPE! HAHA, NO. *THE* RECIPE!

THE RECIPE FOR *THE BEST SALAD IN THE ENTIRE WORLD!!!*

REALLY? WHAT ABOUT THE SARDINIAN TOMATO SALAD?

HMMM, WELL... FOR THOSE OF YOU WHO DON'T HAVE THE OPPORTUNITY TO DISCOVER THIS RECIPE ON THE BACK OF THE STICKER OF THE COOLEST PRODUCT AT THE COOLEST SUPERMARKET...

THAT'S KIND OF A POINTED WAY TO SAY THAT.

HERE IT IS!

Insalata di Patate
(it's the title)

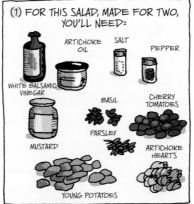

(1) FOR THIS SALAD, MADE FOR TWO, YOU'LL NEED:

ARTICHOKE OIL · SALT · PEPPER · WHITE BALSAMIC VINEGAR · BASIL · CHERRY TOMATOES · MUSTARD · PARSLEY · ARTICHOKE HEARTS · YOUNG POTATOES

(2) MIX TWO TABLESPOONS OF WHITE BALSAMIC VINEGAR AND ARTICHOKE OIL, SOME SALT AND PEPPER, AND ONE TABLESPOON OF MUSTARD IN A SALAD BOWL.

(3) CUT THE POTATOES IN HALF AND STEAM THEM (I LIKE TO USE A POT FULL OF WATER) FOR 15 MINUTES. (POKE THEM TO KNOW IF THEY'RE COOKED, YOU SHOULD USUALLY IGNORE COOKING TIMES IN RECIPES, MOSTLY.)

(HERE, I DREW A STEAM COOKER-- I THOUGHT IT LOOKED NICER.)

(4) MIX (AFTER DRAINING) THE WARM POTATOES WITH THE SAUCE, AND LET THEM COOL.

(5) ADD 3.5 OZ (OR AS MUCH AS YOU WANT) OF CHERRY TOMATOES, CHOPPED FLAT-LEAF PARSLEY, BASIL, AND THE ARTICHOKES FROM THE BOX--CUT IN HALF.

IT WORKS WITH ANY BOX OF ARTICHOKES WITH OLIVE OIL.

AND VOILA! SEE, WASN'T IT WORTH LOOKING ON THE OTHER SIDE OF THE STICKER?

HMM?

CRCHH KLANG! BLING! FOUILLE FOUILLE

UH... ROLAND?

WHAT ARE YOU DOING?

I'M TAKING THE STICKERS OFF OF ALL MY FOOD!

YOU BLEW MY MIND!

CRCHH

I DON'T WANT TO MISS ANOTHER RECIPE!

HA! HA!

MY GOODNESS, ROLAND!

WHAT IS THIS MESS?

IT'S ALWAYS A NICE SURPRISE!

BUT... BUT HEIDI...

CLEAN IT UP!

THIS IS NOT OKAY!

FOUILLE

AND ENJOY!

lon

Pépé Roni's Good Advice: a russe — n° 012

Don't confuse a "panned song"

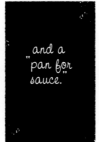

and a "pan for sauce.

BECAUSE ANYONE CAN MAKE MISTAKES!

A russe: a round, slanted pan for sauces.

Eggplant isn't that complicated

TODAY, IN YOUR FRIDGE...

HMMM...

AN EGGPLANT!

NOT BAD!

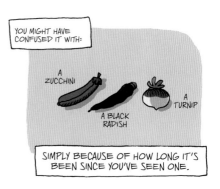

YOU MIGHT HAVE CONFUSED IT WITH:

A ZUCCHINI

A BLACK RADISH

A TURNIP

SIMPLY BECAUSE OF HOW LONG IT'S BEEN SINCE YOU'VE SEEN ONE.

YOU KNOW THAT YOU CAN PREPARE IT IN ON A STOVETOP.

OLIVE OIL

GARLIC

TTSHHH

EGGPLANT

PAPER TOWELS TO SOAK

BUT IT ALWAYS ENDS UP A LITTLE GREASY...

AND THE THOUGHT OF MAKING A RATATOUILLE...

NO THANKS.

FORTUNATELY, FOR YOU, THERE IS: ANOTHER WAY

BAKED EGGPLANT

SIMPLE

RELAXED

DELICIOUS

(1) CUT THE EGGPLANT IN TWO, LENGTHWISE.

AND TAKE OFF THE END.

(2) MAKE AN INCISION WITH THE EDGE OF THE KNIFE FOLLOWING THE SHAPE OF THE EGGPLANT.

THEN SLICE THE SURFACE INTO QUARTERS

MAKE SURE NOT TO CUT THE SKIN!

(3) CUT A CLOVE OF GARLIC IN TWO, REMOVE THE SPROUT.

...SLICE IT INTO STRIPS...

...AND SLIDE THEM INTO THE SLITS OF YOUR EGGPLANT ACCORDING TO YOUR TASTE.

(4) ADD SOME OLIVE OIL, SALT, AND PEPPER.

THEN ADD ANY HERBS YOU LIKE, SUCH AS:

THYME   SAGE   OREGANO   DUCROS©

(AND REPEAT STEPS (2), (3), AND (4) WITH THE OTHER HALF)

(5) FINALLY, PUT THEM INTO A DISH AND BAKE IN THE OVEN AT 400 DEGREES FOR 25 MINUTES.

AND IT'S READY!

IT'S   GOOD!

ENJOY IT NICE AND BAKED, WITH A SPOON, EITHER AS A SIDE DISH OR ENTREE!

lon.

VROOOO

YOU KNOW I WANTED TO ASK YOU ABOUT HOW TO--

EYES ON THE ROAD.

THE NEW FRIEND PART. II

So, I was wondering if you had a trick for--

SHLAFSHLAFSHLAF

stove or in the oven?

If you already answered, can you say it again? I had some water in my ears.

SHLAFSHLAF

Hello?

WELL, NOBODY CAN ACCUSE YOU PROS OF GIVING AWAY YOUR SECRETS EASILY.

IF YOU DON'T WANT--

OKAY LISTEN. UH... YOU'RE STARTING TO ~~DRIVE ME CRAZY~~ TIRE ME OUT, SO I'VE GOT AN OFFER FOR YOU: I'LL GIVE YOU ONE PIECE OF ADVICE AND YOU SHUT YOUR--

DEAL!

HAHA!

OKAY... HERE'S A TIP IF YOU WANT TO MAKE SURE YOU'VE COOKED A PIECE OF RED MEAT, JUST BY FEELING IT.

TSHHHHHH

YOU CAN USE YOUR HAND AS REFERENCE:

(1) TOUCH, WITHOUT PRESSING, YOUR THUMB AND YOUR INDEX FINGER ON ONE HAND AND TOUCH THE FAT OF YOUR THUMB WITH YOUR OTHER HAND:

THAT'S THE FEELING OF BLUE MEAT (OR EXTRA-RARE). IT'S VERY SOFT TO THE TOUCH.

(2) TOUCH YOUR MIDDLE FINGER TO YOUR THUMB AND NOW YOU'VE GOT THE FEEL OF RARE MEAT (YOU'LL SEE PINK JUICE IN THE PAN).

(3) TOUCH YOUR RING FINGER TO YOUR THUMB, AND THAT'S MEDIUM RARE (THE BLOOD WILL SEEP THROUGH THE SURFACE OF THE MEAT).

(4) TOUCH YOUR PINKY FINGER TO YOUR THUMB, AND THAT'S WELL DONE, IT'S FIRM TO THE TOUCH.

BONUS — IF YOU PEPPER THE MEAT ONCE YOU START COOKING IT, YOU'LL GET TOO MUCH HEAT, AND LITTLE FLAVOR. IF YOU PEPPER IT AT THE END, THE PEPPER WON'T TAKE OVER THE DISH AND YOU'LL GET A PLEASANT AROMA.

WOAH...

BUT, HEY! DOES THAT MEAN THAT YOU TOUCH THE--

NOW NOT ANOTHER WORD.

OKAY.

SO, THE POOL?

AWESOME, IT WASH SHO GOOD.

AND THE COOK, IS HE NICE?

I GUESH YOU COULD SHAY WE'RE FRIENDSH!

OH YEAH?

NOM

NOM NOM

YEP

BECAUSE NOW, YOU SEE, WE COMMUNICATE NON-VERBALLY.

SORT OF.

AND YOU SWAM?

DO WE HAVE A STEAK IN THE FRIDGE?

leon.

TODAY LET'S ASK OURSELVES: WHAT DISH CAN PRIDE ITSELF ON BRINGING TOGETHER SOMEONE FROM INDIA, GREECE, SPAIN, AND MOROCCO?

MOVE YOUR BUTTS FOR THE MINISTERS, OR YOU CAN FORGET ABOUT YOUR ID'S!!!

¡JODER!

HAH! NO... I WAS ACTUALLY THINKING OF...

THE ~~FETA~~ WATERMELON SALAD

WATERMELON

FETA

CURRY

MINT

THE RECIPE IS IN THE INGREDIENTS!

(1) START BY CUTTING THE WATERMELON INTO SMALL PIECES:

AND MAKE SURE TO REMOVE THE SEEDS, OF COURSE.

(2) THEN DO THE SAME THING WITH THE FETA:

TIP: CUT THE FETA *IN* ITS PACKAGE (IF YOU BOUGHT IT IN A SUPERMARKET). IT WON'T FALL APART AS MUCH.

(3) MIX THE WATERMELON AND THE FETA IN A SALAD BOWL, CHOP THE MINT AND SPRINKLE IT ON TOP AND THEN SEASON IT WITH A LITTLE CURRY.

THEN PUT IT IN YOUR REFRIGERATOR FOR AN HOUR BEFORE SERVING IT.

OH NO! NO FETA FOR ME!

SOMEONE TOLD ME THAT CHEESE MAKES YOU FAT.

SEND IT BACK.

leon.

bistrot de la Tournelle

5 Petite Place
39600 Arbois

WE FOUND THIS PLACE, BY CHANCE, FOLLOWING THE ADVICE OF A FRIEND TO LOOK FOR A RED DOOR, HIDDEN IN A LITTLE PLACE THAT'S OFTEN DESERTED.

YOU NEED TO GO THROUGH AN EARTHEN HALL, DECORATED WITH SCHOOL POSTERS FROM ANOTHER ERA.

IT'S AN OLD WINE GARDEN AT THE FOOT OF A WALL, BORDERING A RIVER, THAT'S BEEN CONVERTED INTO AN OPEN-AIR BISTRO.

WE DRINK WINES FROM THE REGION: CHARDONNAY, SAVAGNIN OUILLÉ, PLOUSSARD, TROUSSEAU, MACVINE OR YELLOW WINE FOR THREE OR FOUR EUROS A GLASS.

WE EAT FRESHLY BAKED TOAST WITH A CURRY GRATIN, TOASTS WITH TAPENADE, SUN-DRIED TOMATOES, DRY HAM FROM THE NEIGHBORHOOD OR EVEN SNAILS WITH PARSLEY.

A DISCRETE TOAD HAS MADE ITS HOME HERE. IN EVERY CORNER WE CAN HEAR TROUTS SWALLOWING MOSQUITOS FROM THE SURFACE OF THE WATER.

WE HANG AROUND UNTIL LATE INTO THE NIGHT, SPRAWLED OUT IN THE IRON CHAIRS. A GARLAND OF LIGHTS AND CANDLES ARE LIT.

WE TAKE ADVANTAGE OF THE FACT THAT THE AREA IS RELATIVELY UNKNOWN BY TOURISTS AND THAT THE HEAT DOESN'T HIT US AS HARD HERE AS IT MIGHT ELSEWHERE.

PREAMBLE

I'M HANGING OUT IN LAUSANNE, INVITED BY A LIBRARY TO SPEAK ABOUT MY WORK. THAT NIGHT, I LOOK FOR A PLACE TO EAT THAT'S "GOOD AND CHEAP" AND MY LOCAL HOST, *KATIA*, GIVES ME SOME ADVICE OVER THE PHONE:

FROM MEMORY →

ALSO → FROM MEMORY

Yeah, you'll see, behind the Place de la Riponne, there's a small Chinese place run by an old man who used to cook for the Chinese army. There used to be a lot of junkies there, but now it's only Chinese people. I know, I'm not making it sound super appealing, but it's so good. You have to try the noodles. Tell me how you like it.

THE PROMISE

✳ A REAL CHINESE RESTAURANT

✳ NO JUNKIES

✳ CHINESE PEOPLE... MAYBE EVEN BRUCE LEE, WHO KNOWS

✳ A CHANGE OF SCENERY

✳ "TRY THE NOODLES"

OKAY... SO I FIND MYSELF IN FRONT OF... **"CHEZ XU"** (PRONOUNCED "TCHIOO" I BELIEVE) AND, WELL, THE OUTSIDE...

LOOKS LIKE ANY OTHER SWISS BISTRO

10 RUE DU TUNNEL

LET'S BE BRAVE

AND INSIDE, THERE'S:

A WEIRD SORT OF COUNTER TO THE RIGHT WITH:

HA HA

A GUY THAT LOOKS LIKE PHILIPPE LAVIL...

BUT MINUS THE TEETH

HIM   HER   AND HIM

THERE ARE BANQUET TABLES, BUT, SITTING AT THEM...

ONLY JUNKIES

JUNKIES WHO ARE ALL *LOOKING* AT ME

I'M GOING TO DIE.

OH NO, A CHINESE PERSON!

OH NO, HE'S THE CHEF.

HE *LOOKS* LIKE HE WAS IN THE ARMY.

SINCE I DON'T RUN FAST, ANYWAYS, I DECIDE TO GRAB A CHAIR AND SIT DOWN. (MOM STOP READING THIS STORY HERE, PLEASE.)

I REALIZED I HADN'T EATEN CHINESE FOOD OR EATEN ALONE AT A RESTAURANT IN AN ETERNITY.

My god, I hope the waitress speaks French.

THINGS TO DO WHEN YOU EAT ALONE AT A RESTAURANT:

PRETEND TO BE DEEP IN THOUGHT

LOOK AT THE NAPKIN

ROLL UP YOUR SLEEVES

DRINK FROM YOUR GLASS SLOWLY

LOOK FOR SOMETHING

PLAY WITH YOUR CHOPSTICKS (WHEN YOU HAVE SOME)

READ THE MENU THREE TIMES

FIX SOMETHING

AVOID EYE CONTACT

AFTER MUCH HESITATION, I ORDER (EVERYTHING LOOKS REALLY GOOD).

A laminar salad

Okay

Anything else?

You understand?

The "Xu" Soup

Yes

Perfect

...understand what I say?

Of course

And a glass of côtes-du-rhône

no. 6

Yes, yes, I understand

AND I WAIT

THE GLASS OF CÔTES-DU-RHÔNE IS A LITTLE NASTY, AS I EXPECTED. I'M GLAD I DIDN'T ORDER A BOTTLE.

NEXT TO ME, ONE OF THE JUNKIES FOLDS HIS ARMS BACKWARDS.

CRK   CRK

THEN, I SUDDENLY REMEMBER THAT I'M AN ARTIST.

Look at me, I even have a pen on me.

And a real cartoonist draws in their notebook when they're alone, that way they don't have to look at a guy who's folding his arm backwards or sip at their wine for an hour.

WHEN YOU DRAW, YOU ALWAYS MAKE THE SAME FACE THAT THE PEOPLE YOU'RE DRAWING MAKE.

HEHE, THEIR FACES!

UGH, THIS IS KIND OF AN ANNOYING PLACE TO DRAW...

I TAKE OUT A NOTEBOOK AND START DRAWING WHAT YOU'RE CURRENTLY READING.

PLAF!

TEN OR SO MINUTES LATER (I DON'T KNOW HOW LONG EXACTLY, I WAS DRAWING), THE FIRST DISH ARRIVES:

LAMINAR SALAD

HAHA, IT'S FUNNY, IT LOOKS LIKE SEAWEED.

OKAY... ITSH SHEAWEED
CRUNCH CRUNCH CRUNCH

I'M SURPRISED BECAUSE I WAS EXPECTING THE LAMINAR TO BE MUSHROOMS (STRIPS OF THEM) BUT I HAVE TO ADMIT THAT IT'S **VERY** GOOD AND **QUITE** A LARGE PORTION. THE SOUP THAT'S ON IT'S WAY FREAKS ME OUT.

(NEXT TO ME, THE GUY WITH HIS ARMS BACKWARD IS HAVING A DISCUSSION WITH A FRIEND WHILE LAUGHING NERVOUSLY.)

And then his vein starts pissing blood and his eyes begin to roll backwards and ...

THEY'RE DISCUSSING A VIDEO GAME ABOUT SURGERY.

CRUNCH CRUNCH CRUNCH

MY GOD... ALL THIS LAMINAR

AND ALMOST AT THE SAME TIME (AROUND 8 P.M.) A BUNCH MORE HIP-LOOKING PEOPLE ARRIVE.

AND THEN, IT ARRIVES...

HOW WAS IT, SIR?

OH YES, VERY GOOD!

BON APPÉTIT!

QUITE A LOT TO EAT, HUH!

XU SOUP

DO YOU HAVE ROOM? FOR 6

THIS PLACE IS SO CHINESE.

(WHO ARE THESE PEOPLE?)

YEAH, HE'S NOT HERE.

LET'S GO.

Ue!

THE SOUP IS VERY RUSTIC. IT FEELS LIKE THE SORT OF THING YOU'D EAT IN SOME VILLAGE IN THE MIDDLE OF NOWHERE IN CHINA: BOILED BEEF(1), CORIANDER(2), FLAT-LEAF PARSLEY(3), A FEW VEGETABLES(4), AND SOME HANDMADE NOODLES(5). A REAL CHINESE RESTAURANT, AS FAR AS I CAN TELL, ANYWAYS.

AND WHILE I'M EATING, SOMETHING HAPPENS... YOU KNOW THAT FEELING WHEN YOU **REALIZE** THAT YOU ORDERED THE RIGHT DISH AT THE RESTAURANT... THAT JOY...

GOODBYE, NOTEBOOK.

I'D RATHER EAT THAN DRAW!

CHHLRPS

WELL, AS I WAS EATING THIS EXQUISITE SOUP...

...EVERYTHING BECAME MAGICAL, LIKE IN THE OLD **GIGIO** CARTOON.

(I DON'T WANT TO SAY THAT I TRANSFORMED INTO A SEX BOMB, BUT...)

AND THEN...

HAHA, TOO FUNNY!

WOW, THE QUALITY OF THE VENEER ON THE BAR!

SO COOL TO BRING A MAC TO THE RESTAURANT!

B-BUT, YOU DO SPEAK FRENCH!

WOAH

NOO... I WAS DRINKING SAINT JOOO...

NOT POSSIBLE!

HEH, MAYBE THIS ISN'T SALT, BUT **COKE!**

OH SHIT, NO. NOT COKE. NOT...

NOT THE CRUST ON THE...

I ...

WO AH

HEHE, TOO FUNNY. I HAVE TO DRAW THAT GUY AT THE BAR WITH THE DREADS.

THAT FACE

HEY DUDE! IS THAT ME YOU'RE DRAWING, THERE?

STOP BOTHERING HIM, ROGER. **BUT THIS JERK IS MAKING FUN OF US AND DRAWING US!**

LEMME SEE

I'D LIKE THE CHECK PLEASE. QUICKLY.

YOU UNDERSTAND?

I DIDN'T ORDER DESSERT, I HAD ALREADY HAD TOO MUCH TO EAT (THANK GOD). SO, LET'S REVIEW. **VERY** GOOD (IN FACT, THE BEST CHINESE PLACE I'VE EVER EATEN AT), NOT TOO EXPENSIVE (LESS THAN 22 CHF, A BOON IN SWITZERLAND). SURE, IT'S A LITTLE DULL IN COLOR, BUT STILL PRETTY POPULAR.

WOULD I RECOMMEND IT? YES, BUT NOT ALONE.

SIR, YOUR BAG!

Pépé Roni's Good Advice: sauce

n° 069

Don't confuse "feeling saucy"

OOOH... HMMM...

TELLEMENT BOOON ...

and "making sauce."

HMMMM...

SHRLLII

BECAUSE ANYONE CAN MAKE MISTAKES!

Sauce: a cream or liquid served on or used in preparing other foods.

Fall

THE OTHER DAY IN THE SUPERMARKET, YOU HAD A FLASH, A MOMENT OF WEAKNESS--OF CRAZINESS-- DURING WHICH YOU ENTERED THE FOURTH DIMENSION...

THAT IS TO SAY, YOU BOUGHT...

SOME BROCCOLI

PLEASE!

NOW, ALONE IN YOUR KITCHEN, YOU HAVE RETURNED TO REASON, AND YOU ASK YOURSELF:

SHIIIIIT

WHY DID I BUY THIS THING?

DON'T WORRY, IT'S ONLY NORMAL...

YOU RECALL MEMORIES OF SOFT, LUKE-WARM BROCCOLI, FULL OF WATER...

THE VAGUE TASTE OF MOLDY CABBAGE...

WELL, GOOD NEWS: BROCCOLI CAN BE VERY DELICIOUS AND EVEN COOL!

BUT YOU'LL NEED:

BROCCOLI (CAN'T AVOID THAT)

SOY SAUCE

AND MAYBE SOME WASABI PASTE

THEN, YOU NEED TO CUT THE BROCCOLI LIKE THIS:

FOR THE MORE RECKLESS, YOU CAN EAT IT RAW (IT'S SLIGHTLY STRONGER).

I CAN'T BELIEVE I'M GOING TO EAT BROCCOLI!

OR YOU CAN COOK IT IN BOILING WATER FOR TWO OR THREE MINUTES.

BUT IT HAS TO STAY "AL DENTE."

FINALLY YOU SET THE CUT VEGETABLES ONTO A DISH, AND ACCOMPANY IT WITH SAUCERS FULL OF SOY SAUCE, TO WHICH YOU CAN ADD A *LITTLE* WASABI.

TO EAT WARM OR COLD

NOW, **DO NOT** THROW AWAY THE STEM OF THE BROCCOLI! YOU CAN USE IT AS "BONE MARROW" IN A SOUP, OR MIX IT WITH MASHED POTATOES. IT'S DELICIOUS!

OH REALLY?

SO I KEEP EVERYTHING.

LAST PIECE OF ADVICE, AVOID TALKING ABOUT BROCCOLI WHEN YOU SERVE THIS DISH (AS A SIDE TO SOME COLD ROAST BEEF, FOR EXAMPLE) TO YOUR FRIENDS... INSTEAD, INVENT A COOLER NAME LIKE:

THE *BROCOLOUNGE©*.

YOU'LL SEE HOW WELL THE TASTE COMPLEMENTS THE SOY SAUCE!

WOW! IT LOOKS LIKE BROCCOLI!

WOAH!

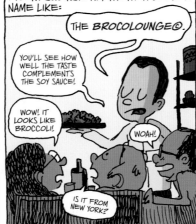

IS IT FROM NEW YORK?

THIS WAS A MESSAGE

FROM THE ASSOCIATION "TURNIPS, CELERY, SPINACH, BRUSSEL SPROUTS, AND OTHER UNFORTUNATE VEGETABLES THAT CAN BE DELICIOUS)"

(T.C.S.B.S.A.O.U.V.T.C.B.D.)

THANK YOU FOR TUNING IN.

leon.

Dear Helene,

I hope that you have made it back safely and that you're enjoying your new studies. I thought about what you asked me the other day when you came to eat at my place, you know... a list of must-have ingredients for your kitchen.

It's complicated because I don't know what you like to cook, so I decided to look in my cupboards to get some ideas. And I decided to write you a letter, rather than just send you an email:

SALT AND **PEPPER** WOULD BE A GOOD START.

(I LIKE GUÉRANDE SALT AND MIXED PEPPER BLENDS.)

YOU CAN EVEN GET SOME LARGE SALT, WHICH YOU'LL USE OFTEN FOR SALTING PASTA WATER, FOR EXAMPLE.

THEN, SOME OIL. MY SOUTHERN ORIGINS PUSH ME TOWARDS ONE SINGLE RELIGION: **OLIVE OIL.** (IT'S GOOD FOR COOKING AND SEASONING MOST DISHES.)

BUT THERE ARE A TON OF OTHER OILS TO DISCOVER... IT'S YOUR CHOICE.

SUNFLOWER NUT ARGAN SESAME RAPESEED

YOU CAN'T FORGET **VINEGAR,** EITHER. WHITE BALSAMIC IS MY FAVORITE: BUT FOR A BASIC VINAIGRETTE, I ALSO HAVE A BOTTLE OF RED WINE VINEGAR (YOU CAN MAKE YOUR OWN WITH MOTHER OF VINEGAR AND WINE... WELL, IF YOU WANT GOOD VINEGAR).

A BOTTLE OF **SOY SAUCE,** TOO, IN CASE OF EMERGENCIES.

THEN FOR THE NON-PERISHABLES, YOU HAVE RICE. INDIVIDUAL BAGS ARE PRACTICAL IF YOU DON'T HAVE A STRAINER, BUT I LIKE BEING ABLE TO TASTE IT, SO THERE'S NOTHING LIKE A BIGGER BAG.

BASMATI, THAI, WILD, RISOTTO, CAMARGUE, JAPANESE... DIFFERENT RICE FOR DIFFERENT DISHES.

I ALWAYS HAVE A THOUSAND TYPES OF **PASTA** AT HOME.

IF YOU DON'T HAVE A LARGE POT, SPAGHETTI CAN GET REALLY ANNOYING. FOCUS ON FUSILLI, PENNE, ORECCHIETTE...

A TOTAL MESS.

HUHU

WELL, IT'S UP TO YOU.

SEMOLINA IS VERY USEFUL, SOMETIMES EVEN FOR BAKING.

AND HERE I WAS WONDERING WHAT TO DO WITH MY CARROTS!

AND I ALWAYS KEEP A BAG OF LENTILS AROUND BECAUSE EVEN THOUGH I DON'T EAT THEM OFTEN, THEY'RE GOOD TO HAVE FROM TIME TO TIME.

FLOUR FOR CAKES OR TO PRETEND TO BE A PRO...

AND **SUGAR.** BOTH THE NATURAL KIND AND POWDERED. (BECAUSE WHAT GOOD ARE THE CUBES FOR, BESIDES RUINING A NICE CUP OF COFFEE, TEA, OR INFUSION?)

IF YOU REALLY WANT TO MAKE CAKES, YOU CAN'T FORGET **YEAST** (IT'S THE SORT OF THING WE BORROW FROM OUR NEIGHBORS ON A SUNDAY NIGHT), AND WHILE YOU'RE IN THE SAME AISLE, BUY SOME **STARCH** (IT'S GOOD FOR THE BAGS OF FONDUE.)

SHOOT.

I MIXED THEM UP AGAIN.

THERE'S ALWAYS A USE FOR **CURRY** AND **CUMIN.**

THEN FOR THE DRIED HERBS, I REALLY ONLY USE **HERBES DE PROVENCE.** THE REST--PARSLEY, CHIVES, ETC.--CAN LOSE THEIR TASTE QUICKLY. THEY'RE BETTER FRESH. BAY LEAVES ARE GOOD IN **SAUCES,** AND **SAGE** IS INCREDIBLE IN THE WATER FOR FRESH PASTA, AMONG OTHER THINGS.

MUSTARD FOR VINAIGRETTES OR WHATEVER ELSE YOU LIKE.

PICKLES? I'M NOT SURE, BUT AT LEAST THEY KEEP WELL.

AND THEN **BOUILLON CUBES** TO USE WITH SUBTLETY.

AS FOR DRY INGREDIENTS THAT ARE ALWAYS USEFUL:

POTATOES

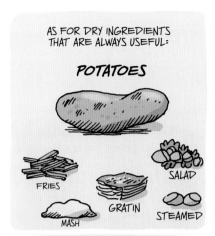

FRIES

SALAD

GRATIN

STEAMED

MASH

AND, NOT FAR FROM THE POTATOES, YOU CAN ALSO FIND **GARLIC, ONIONS, AND SHALLOTS:**

AT THIS POINT IN THE LIST, YOU'LL NOTICE THAT YOU HAVE ALL THE INGREDIENTS YOU NEED FOR A WONDERFUL SUNDAY DINNER OF A SURPRISINGLY CONTROVERSIAL ITALIAN DISH!

GARLIC AND OLIVE OIL PASTA

OH! CANS! VERY THRIFTY...

WHEN I WAS A STUDENT, I ATE SO MUCH CANNED TUNA, ANCHOVIES, MACKEREL, OCTOPUS, ETC. THAT I STARTED TO COLLECT THEM; THAT MADE ME A "CLUPEIDOPHILE."

IF YOU LIKE THEM, THEY'RE REALLY PRACTICAL, AND REALLY GOOD AS FAR AS PRESERVES GO, ESPECIALLY WITH SOME **OLIVE OIL.**

IN MY OPINION, IT'S DIFFERENT FOR MOST OTHER **PRESERVES:** THEY'RE USUALLY DISGUSTING, EXCEPT FOR A FEW EXCEPTIONS SUCH AS:

TOMATOES

CHICKPEAS

CORN

RED BEANS

AND THEY'RE USEFUL TO HAVE, TOO.

IN A LOT OF REFRIGERATORS, YOU CAN FIND **BUTTER, EGGS, AND MILK,** SO DON'T FORGET THOSE.

IN MINE, I ALSO HAVE **LEMON JUICE** (USEFUL) AND I OFTEN HAVE **CREAM,** TOO, THOUGH IT DOESN'T KEEP FOR LONG.

I DON'T KNOW ABOUT YOU, BUT FOR BREAKFAST, I ALWAYS HAVE **TEA** AND **COFFEE.**

AND THREE TONS OF **JAM** THAT MY FAMILY GAVE ME, ALONG WITH SOME NUTELLA©, BUT BE CAREFUL--IT'S VERY ADDICTIVE!

YOU SHOULD ALSO CONSIDER GETTING A BOTTLE OR TWO OF **WINE**... EVEN IF YOU DON'T DRINK ANY, YOU CAN SERVE IT AS AN APPETIZER, USE IT TO DEGLAZE A DISH, OR PLEASE PEOPLE WHO DO DRINK IT.

YOU DON'T NEED TO BUY AN EXPENSIVE BOTTLE, ESPECIALLY IF YOU DON'T HAVE A WINE CAVE.

DID I FORGET ANYTHING? WHILE I WAS LOOKING AROUND, I FOUND SOME **POLENTA,** SOME BOXED **SOUP** (NEVER USED), **COCOA,** A FEW JARS OF **OLIVES** AND A USELESS RABBIT TERRINE.

THAT'S PRETTY MUCH EVERYTHING... OH NO! ONE LAST, REALLY IMPORTANT THING: I ALWAYS HAVE THREE OR FOUR BARS OF **CHOCOLATE** IN THE HOUSE.

(BECAUSE I'VE ALREADY HAD TO BUY SOME AT THE LAST MINUTE ON THE SIDE OF A FREEWAY ON A SUNDAY NIGHT, AND THAT, I ADMIT, DID MAKE ME LAUGH A BIT.)

€6 FOR OFF-BRAND CHOCOLATE?

CAN I HAGGLE?

NO.

There... I hope that this list helps you a little with your groceries. I've done my best not to forget anything, but I'm sure you'll find some things I haven't thought about.

And you'll see, fall is a great season to start cooking. You can still find summer vegetables, next to the new arrivals: squash, mushrooms, chestnuts, cabbage, etc.

I wish you a good start to your new life, and nothing but the best for the rest.
Affectionately,

Guillaume

FOREWORD

CRUNCH

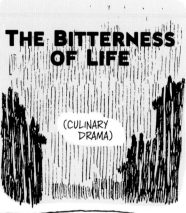

THE BITTERNESS OF LIFE

(CULINARY DRAMA)

THE OTHER DAY I MADE AN **INCREDIBLE** BEEF BOURGUIGNON, AND DESPITE THAT:

ISN'T IT BITTER?

BITTER?

HM? NO

NOT EVEN A LITTLE?

MNOM SCHLURP

THE FOLLOWING DAY, WHILE I WAS EATING A DELICIOUS RATATOUILLE AT MY MOTHER'S:

NOW HOLD ON A SECOND...

WHAT DID YOU PUT IN THIS? WHY IS IT SO BITTER?

EAT YOUR FOOD!

AND AT NIGHT, THE SAME:

EEE!

WHAT'S WITH THESE FRIES?

FRIES SHOULDN'T BE BITTER!

I HAD TO COME TO TERMS WITH IT:

I FIND EVERYTHING BITTER.

EVEN PASTA.

THIS ISN'T NORMAL.

THIS IS SO DEPRESSING...

DO YOU WANT TO DIE?

I SEE, I SEE

NO

SLEEP?

NO

EAT?

NO

LISTEN TO SARDOU?

NO

SAY 33

33

OKAY, WELL NOTHING'S WRONG WITH YOU. THAT'LL BE 33 EUROS.

WHAT'S WRONG WITH ME!!?

(BITTER-TASTING CANDY)

Google

CAUSE OF BITTER TASTE IN MOUTH

SEARCH   I'M FEELING LUCKY

PFFFFF

CLICK

NEWS   SHOP

Google   CAUSES OF BITTER TASTE IN MOUTH

WEB MD LIST THE OPTIONS RESULTING IN THE BITTER

BITTER TASTE FOR THOSE WHO EAT PINE NUTS / ARCHIVES

NUMEROUS PEOPLE ARE COMPLAINING AFTER... INTERNET THE CAUSES OF BITTER TASTE.

BITTER TASTE AFTER

HAHA TOO STUPID!

ABNORMAL TASTE AFTER EATING

THERE ARE PEOPLE WHO EAT PINE NUTS AND WHO--

...

HEY WAIT A SECOND...

CRUN

OH NO!

PINE NUTS

FOR THE LONE FOODIE, A WALK AROUND TOWN ISN'T WITHOUT DANGER...

ASSAULTED BY DELICIOUS SMELLS, HE MUST BE VIGILANT AND STAY THE COURSE.

A GOOD RATATOUILLE, FOR EXAMPLE, AND HIS DEFEAT IS GUARANTEED.

BUT THERE EXISTS AN EVEN MORE INTOXICATING SMELL THAN THE SCENT OF EVEN THE BEST KEBABS...

(I MEAN, WHEN IT'S BEEN A WHILE SINCE YOU LAST ATE AND YOU'VE FORGOTTEN HOW IT CAN SIT IN YOUR STOMACH.)

A SCENT MORE DISTINCT THAN THAT OF WARM BREAD FROM A BAKERY.

ESPECIALLY WHEN YOU HAVE YET TO EAT BREAKFAST.

THE SMELL OF GRILLED ROTISSERIE CHICKEN.

THE CRACKED, SALTY SKIN, SHINING WITH BUTTER... ROTATING SLOWLY AND INEXORABLY...

EVEN THE MOST INTREPID OF GASTRONOMICAL SAILORS...

MOM, THAT MAN IS DROOLING!

DON'T LOOK AT HIM, DARLING! LET'S GO.

...HAVE GIVEN IN TO ITS SIREN CALL.

THE OTHER DAY I WAS DRAWING ANCHOVIES FOR A RECIPE...

PFFF...

WELL, A FILET OF ANCHOVIES...

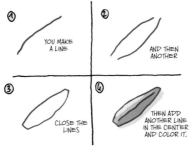

WELL, LET ME TELL YOU: DRAWING AN ANCHOVY FILET IS THE MOST BORING THING IN THE WORLD

① YOU MAKE A LINE

② AND THEN ANOTHER

③ CLOSE THE LINES

④ THEN ADD ANOTHER LINE IN THE CENTER AND COLOR IT.

YOU DON'T EVEN NEED TO SKETCH IT OUT BEFOREHAND.

NOW, I HAVE TO ADMIT THAT ANCHOVIES HAVE KIND OF A BAD REPUTATION.

WHAT'S A SADDER APPETIZER THAN A BOWL OF OLIVES STUFFED WITH ANCHOVIES?

I CAN

SPEAKING OF BAKED OLIVES.... WELL.... NEVERMIND.

NO, NOT PEANUTS!

ME ME!

EVEN ON PIZZAS, IT'S ALWAYS A LITTLE DECEIVING.

FULLY STOCKED ANCHOVIES

WELL, UH... A NEAPOLITAN.

BUT WITHOUT ANCHOVIES.

TAKE MY FRIEND CAROLINE, FOR EXAMPLE: WELL, SHE HATES THEM!

I REFUSE TO EVEN TASTE THEM!

YES I KNOW YOU DON'T CARE THAT I HAVE A FRIEND NAMED CAROLINE, BUT SHE LIKES BEING IN MY COMICS, SO THIS WAS THE RIGHT OPPORTUNITY.

WELL, TOO BAD FOR HER, AND ALL THE OTHERS WHO WILL NEVER KNOW THE PLEASURE:

Orecchiette alla Barese

A PUGLIAN RECIPE

VIVA ITALIA!

FOR THE INGREDIENTS, IT'S SIMPLE, YOU'LL NEED:

ORECCHIETTE (PASTA)

OIL

PECORINO OR PARMESAN

PEPPER

GARLIC

BROCCOLI RABE

A BOX OF ANCHOVIES

SALT

ANNOUNCEMENT: BROCCOLI RABE IS A VEGETABLE PRIMARILY GROWN IN PUGLIA (SOUTHERN ITALY), BUT YOU CAN REPLACE IT WITH... BROCCOLI!

WOW!

THIS IS GREAT! I ALREADY LIKE THIS RECIPE!

PRESIDENT OF THE T.C.S.B.S. A.O.U.V.T. C.B.D.

(1) YOU NEED TO SORT THE BROCCOLI RABE (IT'S THE MOST TIME-CONSUMING PART) AND ONLY KEEP THE LEAVES, THE TENDER STEMS, AND THE FLOWERS.

AND IF YOU'RE COOKING WITH BROCCOLI, WE ONLY KEEP THE FLORETS.

FOR FOUR PEOPLE, YOU'LL NEED ABOUT TWO LBS OF BROCCOLI RABE, OR ONE LB OF BROCCOLI.

AFTERWARD, YOU BOIL SALTED WATER AND COOK THE ORECCHIETTE.

(2) YOU CUT GARLIC AND ANCHOVIES INTO SMALL PIECES, AND GRATE THE PECORINO (IF YOU HAVE THE TIME)...

BECAUSE FIVE MINUTES BEFORE THE PASTA IS COOKED, YOU HAVE TO BE READY TO THROW THE BROCCOLI RABE (OR THE BROCCOLI) INTO THE SAME POT!

(DON'T PANIC, IT'LL REDUCE)

(3) WHILE THE ORECCHIETTE AND THE BROCCOLI RABE FINISH COOKING, BROWN THE GARLIC (SLOWLY SO IT DOESN'T BURN) IN OLIVE OIL ON A STOVETOP.

(USE 5 OR 6 CLOVES FOR 4 PEOPLE)

TSHHHHHH

THEN, WITH THE HEAT TURNED OFF, MELT THE ANCHOVIES WHILE STIRRING (COUNT TEN FILETS FOR FOUR PEOPLE).

(4) STRAIN THE ORECCHIETTE AND BROCCOLI RABE, THEN CONTINUE TO COOK THEM OVER A LOW FLAME FOR TWO MINUTES, WHILE CRUSHING THE VEGETABLES WITH A WOODEN SPOON AND ADDING THE CONTENTS OF THE OTHER PAN AND THE PEPPER.

FCHHHHHH

SERVE WARM, WITH A STRONG GLASS OF RED WINE (WHY NOT A GLASS OF ETNA?) BECAUSE THIS SIMPLE DISH HAS QUITE A STRONG TASTE.

leon.

I WAS NEVER VERY TALENTED WHEN IT CAME TO BAKING... I PREFER SAVORY FOOD OVER SWEETS, AND BESIDES, MEASURING, THERMOMETERS, AND PRECISE TIMING AREN'T REALLY MY THING.

BUT IF THERE IS ONE DESSERT I CAN DO WELL, IT'S:

my chocolate cake

(realistic drawing)

EVERYONE HAS THEIR OWN CHOCOLATE CAKE; SOME ARE FROSTED, SOME ARE POWDERED, OTHERS ARE LAYERED. MINE IS GOOD AND EVEN THOUGH IT'S NOT VERY PRETTY, IT'S **MY** CAKE!

NOW, LET'S THINK ABOUT IT: WHAT DOES A GOOD CHOCOLATE CAKE NEED TO HAVE?

DARK CHOCOLATE, OF COURSE

BUTTER (OR YOU CAN MAKE A YOGURT CAKE)

EGGS

SUGAR, BUT NOT TOO MUCH

WHEN I FIRST STARTED MAKING MY CAKE A FEW YEARS AGO, I USED THE FOLLOWING MEASUREMENTS:

7 OZ OF DARK CHOCOLATE

9 OZ OF SUGAR

5 EGGS

A TABLESPOON OF FLOUR

7 OZ OF BUTTER

but:

It's very sweet and fatty – I can only eat one serving...

SO, I UPGRADED TO THE FOLLOWING RECIPE:

7.5 OZ OF DARK CHOCOLATE

4 OZ OF SUGAR

4 OZ OF BUTTER

and:

yeah yeah... better, but it's not airy enough or soft.

And not pretty.

CHOCOLATE CAKE #2. I MADE IT BY COMBINING A NEW RECIPE WITH THE ORIGINAL UPGRADED VERSION.

NEW

NEW

NEW

5 EGG WHITES BEATEN TO STIFF PEAKS!

1 CUP OF ALMOND FLOUR MINUS THE TABLESPOON OF FLOUR!

ONE BAG OF VANILLA SUGAR!

the result:

it's light

but the inside is still too hard

SO I ADJUSTED THE RECIPE FOR MY CAKE ACCORDING TO THE FOLLOWING:

EXACTLY 18 MINUTES OF COOKING.

OVEN PREHEATED TO 375°F

10-IN SILICONE MOLD

AND DARK CHOCOLATE BAKING BARS THAT ARE EXACTLY 64% COCOA. I ADD A FEW SQUARES OF IT TO THE RECIPE...

and finally:

let's see

CAKE #3 FINALLY HAD EVERYTHING THE IDEAL CHOCOLATE CAKE NEEDS.

Light

chocolate

melts in your mouth

Irresistible taste...

good

wow

But aesthetically, it's just atrocious.

My chocolate cake

THIS IS A RECIPE SEVERAL OF MY FRIENDS HAVE TRIED TO TAKE FROM ME.

BUT, REALLY, I DON'T SEE ANY REASON TO KEEP IT SECRET. IT'S JUST A RECIPE FOR A GOOD CHOCOLATE CAKE.

TO MAKE IT, YOU NEED THE FOLLOWING ~~SECRET~~ INGREDIENTS:

5 MEDIUM CHICKEN EGGS

7.5 OZ OF 64% DARK CHOCOLATE + A FEW EXTRA SQUARES

A PACKET OF VANILLA SUGAR

4 OZ OF SUGAR

4 OZ OF BUTTER

A 10-IN MOLD

1 CUP OF ALMOND FLOUR

(1) START BY PREHEATING YOUR OVEN TO 375°F AND AFTER CUTTING THE 7.5 OZ OF CHOCOLATE AND BUTTER INTO CUBES, MELT THEM DOWN:

(NORMALLY, YOU'D NEED A DOUBLE BOILER, BUT I FIND THAT BOTHERSOME, SO I TURN THE HEAT ON REAL LOW AND I STIR FREQUENTLY AND IT NEVER STICKS.)

(2) BREAK THE EGGS AND SEPARATE THE YOLKS FROM THE WHITES.

KEEP THE WHITES IN A LARGE BOWL AND INCORPORATE THE YOLKS ONE AT A TIME WHILE MIXING INTO THE MELTED CHOCOLATE AND BUTTER.

THEN ADD THE SUGAR, THEN THE ALMOND FLOUR, AND TURN OFF THE HEAT FOR GOODNESS' SAKE!

(3) BEAT THE WHITES INTO STIFF PEAKS IN THE BOWL WITH A PINCH OF SALT (I DIDN'T MENTION THE SALT, BUT YOU DEFINITELY HAVE SOME LYING ABOUT, UNLESS YOU'RE PRONE TO HYPERTENSION, IN WHICH CASE, BEATING THE EGGS BY HAND WILL RELAX YOU)

START AT THE SLOWEST SPEED AND GRADUALLY INCREASE THE SPEED UNTIL THE WHITES FORM STIFF PEAKS

BVRRRR

FOLD THE EGG WHITES **VERY** SLOWLY INTO THE WARM PAN AND TRY TO AVOID BREAKING THEM.

(4) NOW IT'S TIME FOR YOU OR SOMEONE ELSE TO LICK THE PAN.

IT'S AN OBLIGATORY STEP IN THE MAKING OF A CHOCOLATE CAKE.

THEN, POUR A GOOD HALF OF THE EGG WHITE + CHOCOLATE MIXTURE INTO THE SILICON MOLD, AND THROW A COUPLE SQUARES OF THE BROKEN CHOCOLATE ON TOP:

(5) POUR THE REST OF THE MIX OVER IT INTO THE MOLD AND PUT IT IN THE OVEN FOR 18 MINUTES EXACTLY. I'VE PINPOINTED THIS TIME OVER YEARS FOR A MOLD OF THIS EXACT SIZE TO GET **MY** IDEAL CONSISTENCY:

DON'T HESITATE TO ADJUST THE RECIPE ACCORDING TO YOUR MOLD OR THE AGE OF YOUR OVEN.

THIS IS WHERE I AM WITH THIS RECIPE AT THE MOMENT. IN A YEAR OR TWO, I IMAGINE IT'LL HAVE EVOLVED FURTHER.

I'LL LET YOU KNOW.

leon.

the new friend

PART 3

WE'RE GOING.

CHHHT

It feels good to exercise again...

HA! YOU'RE WONDERING WHY I SNICKERED EARLIER.

NO, NOT AT ALL. HOLD ON.

I'LL TELL YOU.

LAST WEEK, I WENT TO AN INCREDIBLE RESTAURANT... INCREDIBLE! I WAS SNEERING BECAUSE I WAS THINKING OF YOUR FACE IF I TOLD YOU WHAT I HAD FOR DESSERT (BECAUSE I KNOW YOU SPECIALIZE IN DESSERTS), SO I HAD A CRAZY *HOMEMADE* MILLE-FEUILLE!

MHM

YEAH... "HOMEMADE" DESSERTS.

PRETTY COOL, RIGHT?

I'M ALWAYS WARY OF MENUS THAT LIST "HOMEMADE" BECAUSE IT IMPLIES THAT THE REST ISN'T.

SO I AVOID THEM.

KEEP MOVING.

NO... TONIGHT, I WAS THINKING WE COULD GO HAVE A HOMEMADE MUSHROOM CRUST AT THE "BALLADIN," AND FOLLOW IT UP WITH SOME HOMEMADE RAVIOLI AT THE "CAFÉ DU CENTRE," BEFORE CLOSING OUT AT THE "REGENT" FOR DESSERT...

MH

MH

THEIR HOMEMADE MILLE-FEUILLE IS THE BEST!

MH

HMF. I THINK WE'LL STAY INSTEAD.

WHERE?

AT HOME.

WHEN IT RAINS IN THE WINTER, I SOME- TIMES THINK OF MY DAD, WHO DIED A FEW YEARS AGO AROUND THIS TIME.

NOT LONG BEFORE HE LEFT, I REMEBER THE SMALL DISCUSSIONS WE HAD ABOUT FOOD...

C-COME CLOSER MY SON...

YEAH, I HAD HAIR LIKE THAT.

SEE HERE, WHEN I WAS YOUR AGE, IT WAS WAR IN THIS COUNTRY, AND THE PEOPLE WERE POOR AND ATE THEIR CHILDREN OUT OF DESPERATION.

SINCE I KNOW YOU LIKE TO EAT, I'D LIKE TO LEAVE YOU A RECIPE AS PART OF YOUR INHERITANCE. I CREATED IT AND FOUND SOME SUCCESS WITH THE GIRLS WHO WERE SPARED BY THE PLAGUE...

THE RECIPE FOR POACHED RAVEN

(ACCORDING TO MEMORY)

(1) THIS IS THE HARDEST PART: YOU NEED TO FIND RAVEN...

Ooh, this one looks pretty good.

(2) HANG IT BY THE NECK IN AN AIRY, DRY AREA.

WHEN THE BODY FALLS OFF ON ITS OWN, IT'S READY!

(3) PLUCK THE BIRD WITHOUT TEARING OFF THE SKIN AND PLUNGE IT INTO A LARGE POT OF BOILING WATER.

(4) ADD A ROCK, SOME LARGE SALT, AND, WHY NOT, A BOUQUET GARNI (BAY LEAVES, THYME, CLOVES, STRUNG IN AN ONION) AND LET IT SIMMER WHILE COVERED.

TUF TUF TUF TUF

(5) POKE THE ROCK FROM TIME TO TIME WITH A FORK: WHEN IT'S TENDER, IT'S FINISHED COOKING!

SHIT, IT'S BEEN TWO DAYS NOW!

PIC PIC

well then...

ACTUALLY, I WONDER IF YOU CAN REALLY EVEN TRUST A RECIPE FROM A GUY WHO DIED FROM COLON CANCER.

lon.

Pépé Roni's Good Advice: blanching — n° 073

Don't confuse "blanching"

and "blanching."

BECAUSE ANYONE CAN MAKE MISTAKES!

Blanching: scalding a raw ingredient in boiling water, to clean it, tenderize it, or remove excess salt.

TRIP TO VENICE

DAY 1

HAS SOMEONE ALREADY SAID, "LEAVING FOR A TRIP IS ALREADY BEING ON A TRIP"? OR DID I COME UP WITH THAT? NOT BAD, IF I DID. WELL, IN ANY CASE, THAT'S THE SORT OF MINDSET WE HAD WHILE WE WERE DRIVING DOWN THE ROAD IN A CONVERTIBLE ON A SWISS FREEWAY...

AT NOON, WE LUNCHED IN A REALLY GOOD JAPANESE RESTAURANT IN LAUSANNE, *PLACE DE LA RIPPONE.*

(NIGIRI, WITH RAW CUTTLE-FISH, A REVELATION)

DURING THE MEAL, MATTHIEU TELLS US ABOUT THE GREAT PIZZAS THAT WE HAVE IN STORE FOR US. IT REMINDS ME OF A RADIO PROGRAM WHERE A JOURNALIST TALKED ABOUT HOW THE FRENCH ARE SPECIALISTS IN TALKING ABOUT FOOD WHILE EATING.

WE KNOW THAT WE'RE *ARRIVING IN ITALY* WHEN NO MATTER WHAT GAS STATION YOU STOP INTO, YOU CAN FIND *REAL COFFEE.*

FORCED TO ADD SUGAR

THERE'S ALWAYS A GUY LIKE THIS AROUND

THE FIRST COFFEE IS SO STRONG THAT I MOMENTARILY LOSE VISION IN MY RIGHT EYE.

FINALLY

WE ARRIVE IN VENICE TOO LATE TO EAT PIZZA. THE ONLY THING OPEN AT THE HOUR IS THE

Mc DONALD'S

AT THE MESTRE RAILWAY STATION

AND, WELL, NOBODY'S HAPPY ABOUT IT.

SILVER LINING

THE "CRISPY BACON" IS BETTER THAN THE "ROYAL BACON" IN FRANCE. *THAT'S IT.*

IT'S THE SORT OF PLACE YOU WANT TO EAT WHEN YOU'VE FORGOTTEN HOW DISGUSTING IT IS AND HOW IT MAKES YOU FEEL AFTERWARD.

I THINK THAT THIS OLIVE BREAD WAS PREPARED IN THE FOLLOWING WAY:

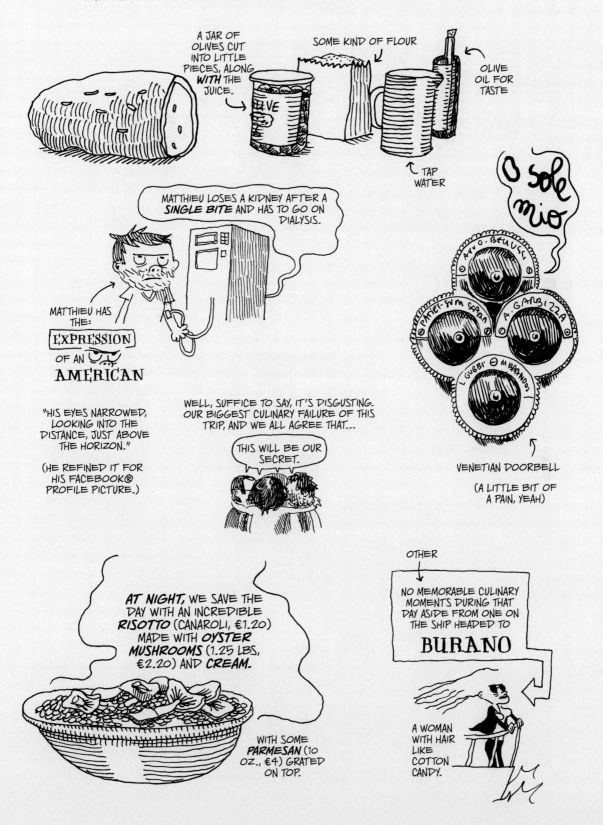

A JAR OF OLIVES CUT INTO LITTLE PIECES, ALONG **WITH** THE JUICE.

SOME KIND OF FLOUR

OLIVE OIL FOR TASTE

TAP WATER

MATTHIEU LOSES A KIDNEY AFTER A **SINGLE BITE** AND HAS TO GO ON DIALYSIS.

MATTHIEU HAS THE: **EXPRESSION** OF AN **AMERICAN**

"HIS EYES NARROWED, LOOKING INTO THE DISTANCE, JUST ABOVE THE HORIZON."

(HE REFINED IT FOR HIS FACEBOOK® PROFILE PICTURE.)

WELL, SUFFICE TO SAY, IT'S DISGUSTING. OUR BIGGEST CULINARY FAILURE OF THIS TRIP, AND WE ALL AGREE THAT...

THIS WILL BE OUR SECRET.

O sole mio

VENETIAN DOORBELL

(A LITTLE BIT OF A PAIN, YEAH)

AT NIGHT, WE SAVE THE DAY WITH AN INCREDIBLE **RISOTTO** (CANAROLI, €1.20) MADE WITH **OYSTER MUSHROOMS** (1.25 LBS, €2.20) AND **CREAM.**

WITH SOME **PARMESAN** (10 OZ., €4) GRATED ON TOP.

OTHER

NO MEMORABLE CULINARY MOMENTS DURING THAT DAY ASIDE FROM ONE ON THE SHIP HEADED TO **BURANO**

A WOMAN WITH HAIR LIKE COTTON CANDY.

DAY 5

THE *RIALTO* MARKET

HEY, GUILLAUME! THERE'S AN OLD LADY WHO'S STEALING TOMATOES!

YOU SHOULD DRAW HER IN YOUR NOTE-BOOK!

IN THE *RIALTO MARKET,* UNDER THE BRIDGES, THERE ARE HEAPS OF FRESH INGREDIENTS FROM THE OCEAN: TURBOT, OCTOPUS, TUNA, SALMON, ST. JACQUES SHELLS, SARDINES, CLAMS, CUTTLEFISH, CRABS, PORGY, RAZOR CLAMS, CRAYFISH, HALIBUT, SHRIMP, BASS, MACKEREL, AND MORE...

WE BUY:

5 SOLES (1.5 LBS)

2.2 LBS OF SICILIAN TOMATOES

1 LB RAZOR CLAMS

2.2 LBS MIXED SALAD (ARUGULA, MESCLUN, ETC.)

1 BOX OF PARSLEY

4-5 SMALL LEEKS

2.2 LBS OF WHITE RAISINS

IN THE STREETS OF VENICE, WE OFTEN PASS BY THIS TOURIST:

IT DRIVES ME CRAZY...

I WANT TO BUY EVERY-THING

FOR LUNCH, WE MAKE:

1) BOIL WATER TO COOK THE FRESH PASTA.

No, but seriously, don't you just feel so good you could cry tears of joy?

4) COOK GARLIC AND PARSLEY IN OLIVE OIL FOR 1 MINUTE. MEANWHILE DESHELL THE RAZOR CLAMS.

2) DISGORGE THE RAZOR CLAMS IN WATER.

AMERICAN EXPRESSION

WINE ↗

MIXED TOMATO SALAD

5) FOR 3 MINUTES, COOK THE RAZOR CLAMS WITH THE GARLIC AND PARLSEY, WHILE THE PASTA COOKS.

3) HEAT THE RAZOR CLAMS FOR 2 MINUTES IN A PAN SO THEY OPEN UP.

TSCHiiiii

TSCHiiiii

FLOPFLOP

NANCY DIDN'T BRING HER SKETCHBOOK, SO SHE USES MINE (AND SHE DRAWS SO MUCH BETTER THAN ME IT HURTS).

I FIND SOME *MARTELLI©* PASTA IN A SHOP, AND IF YOU WANT TO KNOW HOW I FEEL, WELL, IT'S LIKE WHEN INDIANA JONES FINDS THE HOLY GRAIL IN THE THIRD MOVIE (EXCEPT THAT PASTA DOESN'T MAKE YOU AGE FASTER).

AAAH! What did you do in my notebook?

Who's the boss here?

i Maccheroni di Toscana martelli famiglia di pastai dal 1826

TO FINISH SHARING MY ACCOUNT OF THAT DAY, I HAVE TO SPEAK OF THE NIGHT WE SPENT ON THE TERRACE LOOKING AT THE BARGES ON THE CANAL WHILE EATING LEMON-BUTTER GRILLED SOLE, ALONGSIDE A LITTLE RISOTTO WITH SOME SOFT LEEKS, BUT MOST IMPORTANTLY: I'D HAVE TO BE A HELL OF A WRITER TO DESCRIBE, IN JUST A FEW WORDS, EXACTLY HOW DELICIOUS SICILIAN TOMATOES ARE.

I CAN'T BELIEVE IT!

OUR GROCERY BAG STILL STINKS OF THAT OLIVE BREAD!

AT NIGHT WE GIVE IN TO OUR GASTRONOMICAL INDULGENCE BY TREATING OURSELVES TO A NICE LITTLE RESTAURANT.

WE HAVE TO GET THAT OLIVE BREAD OUT OF OUR HEADS.

LA ZUCCA
1762 – SANTA CROCE

ETNA WINE

BROCCOLI

ARUGULA SALAD WITH RAW MUSHROOMS AND PARMESAN

SQUASH WITH PINE NUTS AND PARMESAN FLAN

PISTACHIO SPAGHETTI WITH GORGONZOLA

LASAGNA WITH RED MUSHROOM SALAD

PISTACHIO SPAGHETTI WITH GORGONZOLA

HONEY ALMOND PANNA COTTA

FIOR DI LATTE ICE CREAM AND RED FRUITS

BAVARIAN SQUASH COVERED IN SPICED CHOCOLATE

THE MENU AT

LA ZUCCA

CHANGES REGULARLY AND WAS REALLY VERY, VERY GOOD. I HAVE A GREAT MEMORY OF THE WINE FROM ETNA, WHICH I ALREADY KNEW. WE LEAVE SATIATED, BUT NEVER OVERLY FULL.

AT MATTHIEU'S, FOUR COFFEES. AND AFTERWARD, SOME GRAPPA

"'THE SILENCE AFTER MOZART IS STILL MOZART.' WELL, HERE THE FRESH AIR AS WE LEAVE THE RESTAURANT IS STILL PART OF THE CULINARY EXPERIENCE."

"I'M STILL THINKING ABOUT THAT LASAGNA."

"HERE, YOU CAN BE SURE THIS PASTA WAS AL DENTE."

"AT LA ZUCCA, PUMPKINS TURN INTO CARRIAGES."

AND THEN TO BED.

(WELL, IF I START DRAWING BEAUTIFUL VIEWS NOW, I WON'T BE FINISHING ANY TIME SOON.)

BUT HOW DID WE GET HERE? *AI GRECI*, A TOURISTY RESTAURANT IN THE *CASTELLO* NEIGHBORHOOD. I WANT TO DIE. THE WAITERS LOOK INDIAN, SPEAK ENGLISH, FRENCH, SPANISH, GERMAN, AND ITALIAN, AND THERE'S A BUDDHA IN THE CORNER.

DAY 7

IT SMELLS LIKE MOLDY BREAD FOR SIX MILES AROUND, AND I'M FEELING A LITTLE BUMMED OUT, BECAUSE I KNOW IT'S MY SECOND TO LAST MEAL IN VENICE AND YESTERDAY WAS AN EXCEPTIONALLY DELICIOUS DAY... ALL BECAUSE:

(BEHIND US THERE'S A FRENCH FAMILY WHO ARE VERY PLEASED WITH THEIR MEAL.)

WOW! LOOK AT THE SIZE OF THE PIZZAS!

IT'S ITALY!

5.5 INCHES IN DIAMETER, 3 DEAD FISH ON TOP.

THE GIRL SAYS:

THIS IS THE BEST PIZZA I'VE EVER HAD!

THE PIZZA IN QUESTION IS VERY STIFF AND STRAIGHT.

3 DAYS AGO — I WANT PASTA AL NERO DI SEPIA

2 DAYS AGO — I WANT PASTA AL NERO DI SE

YESTERDAY — PASTA AL NERO DI SEP

SO MATTHIEU SAYS, "OKAY, WE'RE GOING TO EAT THE BEST PASTA AL NERO DI SEPPIA*, ACCORDING TO MY DAD."

* SQUID INK PASTA

EXCEPT THAT THEN, MATTHIEU CALLS HIS FATHER TO BE SURE HE'S GOT THE RIGHT ADDRESS.

AND STILL THAT AMERICAN EXPRESSION...

You're sure of yourself, right?

Because this place looks terrible.

Yeah, Castello, that's it.

AND FINALLY:

IT'S GOOD

BUT IT'S THE ONLY THING WE CAN ORDER.

UNCOMFORTABLY, WE ORDER A CARAFE OF WATER, FOUR PASTA AL NERO DI SEPPIA, AND, JUST FOR GOOD MEASURE, A VINEGAR SARDINE.

WATER

PASTA

BREAD

BREADSTICKS

AS PROMISED, THE SARDINE IS DISGUSTING.

BUT THE PASTA'S DEFINITIVELY DELICIOUS, SO IT WAS WORTH THE RISK.

WHEN YOU EAT THIS PASTA, YOUR LIPS AND TEETH TURN BLACK AND IT MAKES YOU LOOK GOTH. →

AFTERWARD, WE HAVE SOME GELATO--SQUASH, CHOCOLATE PEAR, AND FIOR DI LATTE E CIOCCOLATO

DAY 8

(RETURN TO FRANCE)

IN ONE OF THE FREEWAY SERVICE STATIONS, WE HAVE A SMALL PICNIC BETWEEN TWO TRUCKS. WE EAT SOME SPECK, ITALIAN CHEESE, SUN-DRIED TOMATOES, AND PEPPERS MARINATED IN SICILIAN TOMATOES...

ITALY DOESN'T TASTE QUITE THE SAME WHEN IT'S NOT IN ITALY.

SO I ASK MYSELF SOMETHING:

(1) WHY IS IT THAT IN FRANCE THE COFFEE IS DISGUSTING IN MOST BISTROS, RESTAURANTS, ETC., WHILE IN ITALY IT'S PERFECT-- EVEN AT A SERVICE STATION? ARE OUR PERCOLATORS THAT MUCH WORSE? OUR COFFEE?

(2) WHY IS THE BEST PASTA (DRY) WE CAN FIND IN FRANCE NEVER AS "AL DENTE" AS THE PASTA FROM, FOR EXAMPLE, THE COOP, THAT YOU GET IN ITALY? DOES THE DENSITY CHANGE WHEN IT CROSSES THE BORDER? IS THEIR FLOUR BETTER?

AT THE SAME TIME, ACROSS THE FREEWAY:

WHY IS OUR BREAD SO BAD WHEN IN FRANCE IT'S SO GOOD?

AND WHY DO WE ADD THE JUICE FROM A JAR OF OLIVES?

END OF THE TRIP

Winter

ONE FINE DAY...

OR MAYBE ONE NIGHT...

I FELL ASLEEP NEAR A FIELD.

WHEN, SUDDENLY, OUT OF NOWHERE, A BLACK RADISH SEEMED TO BURST FROM THE EARTH!

SLOWLY, THE LEAVES SPREAD APART, CALLING ME.

THE SCENT OF TURNIPS.

AS I WAS SWEATING, IT BEGAN TO CRAWL.

IT WAS COVERED IN DIRT, ITS SKIN THE COLOR OF THE NIGHT.

ON ITS SIDE THERE WAS A BITE MARK, LIKE A SCAR.

I BRAVELY TOOK A BITE OUT OF IT, JUST TO SEE HOW IT TASTED.

THAT'S WHEN I RECOGNIZED IT:

SURGING FROM MY PAST, IT CAME BACK TO ME!

OH RADISH, NO! DON'T TAKE ME WITH YOU TO ANOTHER TIME!

ALL THAT TIME AGO, IN THE SCHOOL CAFETERIA

WHERE I SO FEARED YOUR BITTER TASTE!

JUST LIKE BEFORE, LIKE IN MY NIGHTMARES... LIKE BEFORE, STUCK IN MY CHAIR.

JUST LIKE BEFORE, I HAD TO FINISH EVERYTHING AND EVEN DRINK YOUR JUICE IN ORDER TO LEAVE!

THE RADISH STARED AT ME FROM THE GROUND, LAUGHING AT ME WHILE I RECOILED.

I SPIT UP THE FOUR PIECES I HAD HALFWAY-CHEWED.

I WAS HUNGRY, AND I HAD NOTHING LEFT. THE MCDONALD'S NEARBY HAD ALREADY CLOSED!

ONE FINE DAY OR WAS IT NIGHT?

I FELL ASLEEP NEAR A FIELD WHEN, SUDDENLY, OUT OF NOWHERE

A BLACK RADISH SEEMED TO BURST FROM THE EARTH!

Endives are bitter.

ENDIVES

Candied with oranges

AND FRIED SCALLOPS

STARRING

(FOR TWO)

We'll see about that!

one large orange

fresh coriander (optional)

BUY US FRESH!

WE DON'T HAVE ANY TASTE FROZEN!

Four beautiful king scallops

two great endives

salt and pepper

butter

sugar

(1) PLUCK THE ENDIVES

PRESS THE ORANGE

PLUCK THE CORIANDER

THE QUANTITY IS UP TO YOU

(2) IN A LARGE PAN, HEAT SOME BUTTER (ABOUT 3 TABLESPOONS) AND 2 TABLESPOONS OF SUGAR

LET IT CARAMELIZE

TSHH   FLFLFSH

THEN DEGLAZE WITH THE ORANGE JUICE

TSHSHHSHHHH

(3) COOK THE PLUCKED ENDIVES IN THE ORANGE JUICE ON A LOW HEAT AND COVER FOR 15-20 MINUTES

FFFFFFF

YOU'LL KNOW THE ENDIVES ARE READY WHEN THEY TURN A LITTLE TRANSLUCENT OR THE SAUCE HAS COMPLETELY REDUCED.

KEEP WARM.

HUHU!

(4) IN A SMALL PAN, MELT SOME BUTTER OVER A HIGH HEAT, UNTIL IT BROWNS.

QUICKLY ADD THE SHALLOTS, FOR NO MORE THAN 2 MINUTES ON EACH SIDE.

I'M GOING TO GET YOU!

EEEEEEK!

(5) SEASON WITH SALT AND PEPPER AND SERVE THEM IN A PLATE WITH THE ENDIVES AND THEIR JUICE. SPRINKLE SOME FRESH CORIANDER ON TOP AND MAKE IT LOOK FANCY!

WE'RE NOT CHEAP, WE KNOW...

BUT TREAT YOURSELF SOMETIMES!

"CRISPY AND SOFT AT THE SAME TIME"

SOOOO, EH? STILL TASTE BITTER?

NO, IT'S FINE NOW, BUT I DON'T LIKE SURIMI!

HEH.

HONESTLY, I WAS NEVER ALL THAT GOOD AT MAKING CREPES:

DAMN IT!

TOO SOFT OR TOO LIQUIDY...

SPLATCH!

TOO HARD OR THICK...

SIR?

ARE YOU OKAY?

SO, AFTER 30 YEARS, I DECIDED TO CONFRONT THE PROBLEM:

Yes yes...

What?

Oh really? Brittany is in France?

Okay, thank you!

Hey, Arnaud? Guess who it is.

No No... No What if I said 6e?

no not that either

yes? no!

noo

COOKING LESSON FROM A BRETON

KENVAVO!

I'M ON MY WAY!

TO START, "KENVAVO" MEANS "GOODBYE"...

BUT COME INSIDE.

LET'S MAKE SOME CREPES.

OK, FIRST... FORGET ALL ABOUT "3 EGGS, 1 CUP FLOUR, 2 CUPS MILK." WE'RE MAKING CREPES WITHOUT MEASURING!

WITHOUT MEASURING?

YEAH.

NEED ME TO SAY IT AGAIN?

UH OH. REALLY, I CAN'T MEASURE?

WELL, WE CAN MAKE THE STUPID CREPES YOU FLIP IN THE PAN,

BUT I'VE NEVER SEEN A BRETON FLIP A CREPE.

NEVER?

NEVER.

NEVER...

NEVER.

SECOND THING: THERE ARE AS MANY CREPE RECIPES AS THERE ARE BRETONS!

WOAH...HOW MANY BRETONS ARE THERE?

MILLIONS.

WHAT!?

AND ME, IN MY RECIPE, I ADD...

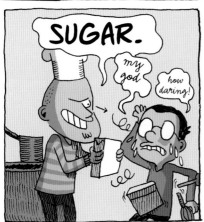

SUGAR.

my god

how daring!

YES, I KNOW... IT CAME TO ME SUDDENLY AFTER SEVERAL YEARS... ADDING A LITTLE BIT OF SUGAR TO THE BATTER, MAKES IT... A LITTLE FIRMER, MORE ELASTIC...

WELL, IT STICKS A LITTLE MORE, TOO.

BUT HAVE YOU EVER SEEN A BRETON FLIP A CREPE?

BÔM!

NEVER.

OKAY... ENOUGH TALK.

ARE WE MAKING CREPES OR WHAT?

I CAN'T HEAR YOU!

LET'S MAKE THEM.

THERE... I PUT A RAG TO PROTECT THE BATTER... WE'LL HAVE TO STIR IT A LITTLE BEFORE WE MAKE THE FIRST CREPE.

WE WAITED FOR SO LONG!

WELL... IT WAS NECESSARY FOR THE FLOUR TO ABSORB THE MILK...

PASS ME THE CREPE PAN BEHIND YOU.

YOU DON'T USE A BILLIG?

OH NO!

NOT FOR SWEET CREPES...

I ONLY USE MY BILLIG FOR MY BUCKWHEAT CREPES.

OH REALLY?

BY THE WAY, YOU DON'T CALL IT A GALETIERE?

HAVE YOU EVER EATEN IN A GALETTERIE?

UH, WELL... NO.

WELL THEN.

SCRATCH SCRATCH

FORGET ABOUT BILLIGS AND GALETIERES!

THE IMPORTANT PART IS TO HAVE A CREPE PAN *THAT YOU DON'T USE FOR ANYTHING ELSE:*

YOU HAVE TO RESPECT CREPES!

THEN, YOU LET THE PAN HEAT UP WITH JUST A LITTLE BIT OF OLIVE OIL THAT YOU SPREAD WITH:

FORK

HAND

POTATO CUT IN HALF

PAPER TOWEL

AFTER, YOU POUR A LITTLE BIT OF THE CREPE BATTER INTO YOUR HOT PAN... WHEN THE EDGES OF THE CREPE TURN GOLDEN, IT'S TIME TO TURN IT AROUND!

TCHHHH

YOU CAN USE A SPATULA, BUT I USE MY HANDS!

REDUCE THE HEAT FOR THE OTHER SIDE

OW

FEAT

YOU ALWAYS HAVE TO TASTE... NOM CHLURP GRUB THE FIRST CREPE, SINCE YOU'RE COOKING WITHOUT MEASURING. IF THE BATTER IS TOO THICK, YOU CAN ADD MORE MILK.

I SEE

GLP!

BUT HERE, IT'S *PERFECT*

I SEE...

TSHHH

THAT SAID, WHEN YOU'RE ADDING MILK, MAKE SURE NOT TO SURPASS THE FAMOUS...

BREAK POINT LIMIT

of crepe batter

BECAUSE IF IT GETS TOO WET, YOUR CREPES WILL TURN OUT LIKE CRAP AND YOU'LL HAVE TO THROW OUT YOUR BATTER.

(YOU CAN TRY TO FIX IT BY MIXING AN EGG TOGETHER WITH SOME FLOUR IN A BOWL AND REINTEGRATING THAT WITH THE REST OF YOUR BATTER, BUT IT'S NOT A SURE THING.)

WHEN ALL THE CREPES ARE DONE, DON'T FORGET TO LEAVE YOUR BOWL TO SOAK, OTHERWISE IT'S A PAIN TO CLEAN UP AFTER.

OKAY

I GET IT.

GROOO

AND IF YOU DON'T HAVE *TOO* MANY CREPES (THOUGH CAN YOU *NEVER* REALLY HAVE TOO MANY CREPES) YOU CAN KEEP THEM FOR A DAY IN A CLOSED OVEN WHILE OFF, BUT BE SURE NOT TO STUFF THEM IN THE REFRIGERATOR!

I UNDERSTAND

NOW ALL THAT'S LEFT IS TO--

THERE, NOW I'VE MADE MY PORTION OF THE CREPES! YOU SEE, IT'S NOT THAT COMPLICATED!

...

THERE'S JUST A FEW THINGS TO WATCH OUT FOR.

THERE ARE SOME EGGS AND MILK IN THE FRIDGE IF YOU WANT TO GIVE IT A GO!

I UNDERSTAND

NOM CHLURP GRUB

lon.

THERE'S THIS SONG THAT PLAYS ON THE RADIO FROM TIME TO TIME...

...THE GOVERNMENT SUGGESTS 30 FRUITS AND VEGETABLES PER DAY.

AS A RESULT, YOU STUPIDLY BOUGHT:

"AND SUDDEN-LY... NA NA NA... BURSTING FROM THE EARTH... NA NA NA..."

"BLACK RADISH OUT OF NO-WHERE..."

a black radish

WHOA LA LA LA LA

AND NOW YOU'RE EMBARKING ON A NEW ADVENTURE WITH A SINGLE QUESTION AT ITS CORE: WHAT DO I DO WITH THIS?

START BY PEELING IT, THE SKIN ISN'T EDIBLE.

AND REMOVE THE LEAVES.

WHAT!?

IT'S ALL WHITE!

THE FIRST WAY IS THE EASIEST:

TRUE, BUT IT'S STILL A BLACK RADISH.

RADISH
BREAD BUTTER SALT

CUT THEM INTO RINGS

SAUSAGE

BOURSIN® CHEESE

AND EAT IT **RAW**, WITH BREAD OR WHATEVER YOU PREFER

NOTHING...

HMM SIMPLE...

BUT IT'S SO STRONG!

SECOND WAY, SLICE IT EVEN MORE FINELY (WITH A REALLY GOOD KNIFE OR A PEELER) AND EAT IT IN A SALAD:

NORMAL SLICE

EXTRA-THIN SLICE

RADISH SALT SESAME SEEDS
OLIVE OIL
PEPPERS LEMON PEPPER

OR JUST GO AHEAD AND GRATE IT TO HAVE WITH SALMON OR TUNA SASHIMI (OR OTHERS).

FISH

BLACK RADISH SOY SAUCE

WASABI

IF YOU'D LIKE TO STICK TO THE RAW RADISH, YOU CAN ALSO DISGORGE* IT WITH SOME LARGE SALT, SO IT GIVES LESS WATER IN THE SALAD.

OH GREAT

COULDN'T YOU HAVE TOLD ME THIS **BEFORE?**

(* SPRINKLE THE SLICED RADISH WITH LARGE SALT (FOR EXAMPLE, KOSHER SALT), AND LET IT REST FOR 1/2 HOUR TO AN HOUR, REMOVE THE WATER AND WIPE DOWN THE SLICES WITH A CLEAN RAG)

BLACK RADISH SOUP

YOU'RE TIRED OF THOSE LAME APPETIZERS YOU'RE USUALLY SERVED. YOU'VE HAD ENOUGH OF MIXED NUTS, CASHEWS, AND EVEN GRILLED PEANUTS. THEY'RE NOT WHAT THEY USED TO BE. YOU'RE TIRED OF THE VERRINES, "TRENDY" AMUSE-BOUCHES, AND, IN ANY CASE, THEY TAKE TOO LONG TO MAKE FOR AN APPETIZER!

CHIPS & GUACAMOLE!

WELL, **GOOD NEWS** FOR YOU. HERE ARE A FEW IDEAS TO HELP YOU MAKE SOME DELICIOUS APPETIZERS QUICKLY AND WITH JUST A FEW INGREDIENTS.

A FEW QUICK APPETIZERS

THAT DON'T TAKE LONG TO MAKE

YOU'RE SAYING PEANUTS AREN'T ENOUGH?

I HAVE TO COOK APPETIZERS, TOO?

DON'T TAKE LONG...

I WOULD SAY IT DEPENDS ON THE QUANTITY

(WARNING: EAT IMMEDIATELY BECAUSE IT GIVES OFF QUITE A LOT OF WATER. OF COURSE, IF YOU'D LIKE, YOU CAN SWEAT AND SALT THE ZUCCHINI BEFOREHAND TO DISGORGE IT, AND THEN PUT IT IN THE OVEN TO DRY, BUT WHY BOTHER? IT'S SO MUCH BETTER FRESH!)

④ WHITE ITALIAN GRAPES

CUMIN GOUDA

TOOTHPICKS

REMOVE THE SEEDS

CUT INTO CUBES

MAKE SKEWERS

⑤ PRUNES

BACON

TOOTHPICKS

ROLL THE PRUNES INTO THE BACON

MAKE SKEWERS

PUT IN THE OVEN AT 425°F FOR A MOMENT

⑥ CUCUMBER CUT IN TWO

MUSHROOMS, PEELED AND DE-STEMMED

AND PEELED

HOLLOW OUT THE CUCUMBER, REMOVE THE SEEDS WITH A SPOON

BOURSIN® CHEESE

FILL THE MUSHROOMS AND CUCUMBER WITH CHEESE

(PACK IT IN)

⑦ SHELLED SHRIMP

TOOTHPICKS

OIL

GRILL IN A PAN

ASSEMBLE

ADD MINCED GARLIC

CHOPPED PARSLEY AT THE END

(MAKE SURE NOT TO BURN)

⑧ COOKED SHELLED SHRIMP

SLICED BLACK RADISH

MINT LEAVES

LARGE SALT

TOOTHPICKS

⑨ BOXED WHITE BEANS

OLIVE OIL

LIME JUICE

TAHINI

TABASCO

BVVZVZVVVV

ENDIVE

FIGS

PROSCIUTTO

GUERANDE
SALT

BALSAMIC
VINEGAR

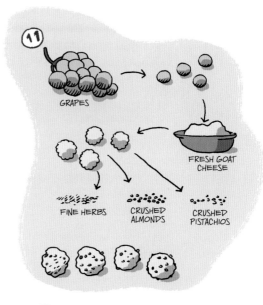

GRAPES

FRESH GOAT
CHEESE

FINE HERBS

CRUSHED
ALMONDS

CRUSHED
PISTACHIOS

SPINACH LEAVES

VINAIGRETTE
(OIL, VINEGAR,
MUSTARD, SALT,
PEPPER)

RAW
HAM

(ROLL IT UP)

ENDIVE

ROQUEFORT©
NUT

BOURSIN®

CREME FRAICHE -
SHALLOTS - VINEGAR
- BALSA - CHIVES

CARROTS
KIWI

LEMON
TAPENADE

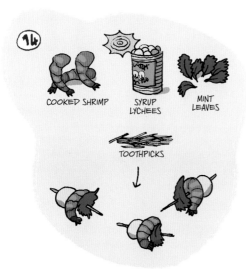

COOKED SHRIMP

SYRUP
LYCHEES

MINT
LEAVES

TOOTHPICKS

COMTÉ*
CHEESE
CUT INTO
STRIPS

BREAD CUT INTO SLICES

*GOOD

SPRINKLE WITH
CURRY POWDER

PUT ON
BREAD

GRILL
A BIT

MID-MARCH IS FERA SEASON. SO, STUPIDLY, YOU SAY:

I'LL HAVE SOME FERA TO...

HINHIN

TO UH... MAKE A... TARTAR!

AND HERE, EQUALLY STUPIDLY, THE FISHMONGER (YES, THE FERA IS A FISH) WILL SAY:

HERE'S YOUR FERA.

BON APPETIT

IN EFFECT, NEITHER OF YOU REALIZE HOW DIFFICULT IT IS TO FIND FERA FOR THE SIMPLE REASON THAT...

FERA NO LONGER EXISTS!

OH REALLY?

WHAT DID I BUY THEN?

EH?

TO ANSWER THIS QUESTION, LET US TAKE LOOK BACK IN TIME TO THE MONTH OF DECEMBER OF AN UNKNOWN YEAR WHEN THE FERA ENJOYS ITS DAYS IN SWITZERLAND IN LAKE GENEVA'S GLACIAL WATERS...

Merry Christmas, Jean-Jacques

500 KILOMETERS FROM HERE, IN DECEMBER OF THE YEAR 1930, JEAN FERRAT WAS BORN... NO RELATION, BUT HERE COMES THE UNNECESSARY WORDPLAY...

AND YET...

QUICKLY, HE FINDS SUCCESS BY SINGING A FEW POPULAR SONGS.

POURTAAAN...

QUE LA MONTAGN EST BEEUEU

THE FERA, ON THE OTHER HAND, DOESN'T SING, OR SINGS POORLY. IT'S HARD TO TELL UNDERWATER:

ONE DAY, A GUY NOTICES THAT FERA IS DELICIOUS.

GRÜTLI!

ON HIS END, JEAN FERRAT ENJOYS A WELL-DESERVED RETIREMENT.

HEY, GIRLS!

WHAT IF I JOINED THE F.C.P.*?

HEHE!

YEAAH!

* FRENCH COMMUNIST PARTY

AFTERWARD, HE DIES, AND BECAUSE HE'S WELL KNOWN, THE PRESIDENT OF FRANCE GIVES A SPEECH.

WELL...

HE WAS A REALLY GOOD GUY!

EXCEPT FOR THE WHOLE THING WITH THE F.C.P.!

HEH!

HAHA!

TOGETHER

YES! WELL SAID!

YES!

THE FERA, VICTIM OF ITS SUCCESS, ALSO DISAPPEARS, BUT NOBODY GAVE ANY SPEECHES ABOUT IT:

BÛÛURP!

WELL, THAT FERA WAS DELICIOUS, I'D LOVE ANOTHER.

THERE'S NO MORE.

WELL, I'LL COME BACK.

NO, THERE AREN'T ANY LEFT *AT ALL.*

...EXCEPT THAT WE'RE IN... *1920!* TEN YEARS BEFORE THE BIRTH OF JEAN FERRAT!!

SO, TEMPORAL PARADOX OR A SIMPLE COINCIDENCE? REINCARNATION OR SUPERSTITION? A NEW SPECIES ALWAYS REPLACES THE ONE BEFORE IT, AND IN 1921 IT WAS...

THE JEAN-FERA OF THE LAKE!

YOU CAN TELL THE JEAN-FERA OF THE LAKE FROM THE FERA DUE TO TWO DISTINGUISHING FEATURES: IT'S CAPABLE OF SWIMMING AGAINST THE CURRENT, AND IT HAS A SORT OF MUSTACHE THAT FISHERMAN GENERALLY CUT OFF WHEN THEY CATCH IT:

TODAY, OUT OF HABIT, PEOPLE CONTINUE TO CALL THIS FISH "FERA."

SERIOUSLY?

YOU'RE NOT MESSING WITH ME ARE—

AIMEER A'EN PEERDRE LA RAISOON

DID *YOU* JUST SING?

?!

SING WHAT?

OH JEAN FERRAT SONGS ARE SO CATCHY!

FORGET IT!

HOPEFULLY THIS WON'T KEEP YOU FROM FINISHING YOUR GROCERY SHOPPING!

THAT STORY IS CRAZY!

MA MÔME ELLE JOUE PAS LES STARLETTES

IT'S NICE OUT TODAY AND IT'S THE PERFECT OCCASION TO MAKE A DELICIOUS...

JEAN-FERA OF THE LAKE TARTAR

FRESH FILET OF JEAN-FERA (3.5 OZ PER PERSON, GENERALLY)

FILET OF SMOKED JEAN-FERA (A LITTLE LESS PER PERSON THAN THE FRESH)

ARUGULA

SALT

PEPPER

CHIVES

LIME

SHALLOTS

NORMAL OIL. SUNFLOWER, FOR EXAMPLE

NUT OIL

MUSTARD (WITH SEEDS, IT'S BETTER)

BALSAMIC VINEGAR

IT'S GOOD!

BUT THAT STORY IS REALLY CRAZY...

(1) CUT THE SMOKED AND FRESH FILLET INTO CUBES AND MAKE SURE THERE AREN'T ANY BONES

IF YOU DECIDED TO GO AHEAD AND BUY THE FISH WHOLE,

WELL, GOOD LUCK GETTING THE BONES OUT AND FILLETING THEM. I DON'T KNOW HOW TO DO IT.

AFTERWARD, THE CUBED FISH GOES DIRECTLY INTO THE FRIDGE, OR EVEN THE FREEZER, UNTIL YOU'VE FINISHED PREPARING THE REST.

(2) FOR THE VINAIGRETTE, YOU'LL NEED THIS MUCH PER PERSON:

THE JUICE FROM 1/4 OF A LEMON

1 TABLESPOON OF OIL

1 TABLESPOON OF NUT OIL

1/2 TABLESPOON OF BALSAMIC VINEGAR

1 TEASPOON OF MUSTARD

AND MIX WELL. THE IDEA IS TO HAVE A VINAIGRETTE THAT DOESN'T TASTE TOO STRONGLY OF NUTS.

(3) POUR THE VINAIGRETTE OVER THE CUBES OF JEAN-FERA AND PUT THEM BACK IN THE FRIDGE FOR 15 MINUTES.

(THEY NEED TO SOAK A LITTLE, TO ABSORB THE VINAIGRETTE.)

THEN, FINELY CHOP THE CHIVES AND SHALLOTS. THE QUANTITY IS UP TO YOU.

(4) ON THE PLATE, MAKE A SMALL BED OF ARUGULA.

SPREAD THE JEAN-FERA TARTAR OVER TOP SO IT LOOKS NICE:

SEASON WITH THE CHIVES, SHALLOTS, SALT AND PEPPER, A FINAL DRIZZLE OF NUT OIL AND VOILA.

A NICE GLASS OF WHITE JURA WINE LIKE A SAVAGNIN OR CHARDONNAY WILL COMPLETE THE PAIRING!

lon.

Pépé Roni's Good Advice: a chef's knife

n° 601

Don't confuse "work/life balance"

and "work/knife balance."

BECAUSE ANYONE CAN MAKE MISTAKES!

A chef's knife: knife most commonly used by chefs in the kitchen. good for cutting both meats and vegetables.

MY NEW FRIEND IV

(1) YOU SHOULD USE TWO EGGS PER PERSON... FIRST CHALLENGE, USING THE RIGHT PAN:

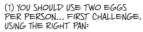

TOO BIG AND THE OMELET WILL BE TOO THIN AND DRY.

TOO SMALL, AND YOU'LL HAVE A POORLY COOKED EGG PUREE...

NEXT, YOU DON'T BEAT YOUR EGGS OR ELSE THEY'LL FORM A MOUSSE, AND WITH ALL THE AIR YOU'LL HAVE INCORPORATED, YOUR OMELET WILL INFLATE AND YOU'LL BE BETTER OFF USING IT AS A WINDOW SEAL.

(2) INSTEAD, MIX THE EGGS ROUGHLY IN A BOWL, WITH A FORK, FROM TOP TO BOTTOM.

ADD SALT, PEPPER, AND HERBS IF YOU LIKE.

THEN, HEAT A LITTLE BIT OF BUTTER OR OIL IN YOUR PROPERLY SIZED PAN, AND ONCE IT'S NICE AND HOT, POUR THE EGGS INSIDE.

FLFLFLCHHHH

(3) THIS IS THE MOST IMPORTANT PART: WAIT UNTIL YOUR OMELET FORMS A LITTLE, THE EDGES WILL BECOME A LITTLE OPAQUE, AND THEN, WITH A WOODEN SPATULA, PULL YOUR OMELET IN FROM THE SIDES TOWARDS THE CENTER AGAIN AND AGAIN.

COOKED EDGES

LIQUID CENTER

(4) YOUR OMELET WILL LOOK LIKE A SMALL PIT WITH A VISCOUS CENTER... SO TILT THE PAN AND FOLD THE OMELET ON ITSELF WITH THE SPATULA:

AND THEN YOU'LL HAVE A THICK, RUNNY, CREAMY OMELET THAT YOU CAN KEEP COOKING ACCORDING TO TASTE.

IN THE HEART OF WINTER, WHEN THE COLD GRIPS YOUR CHEEKS AND FREEZES YOUR TOES...

NOW THAT'S A GOOD LINE

I'LL USE IT AGAIN.

THERE'S ALWAYS A MOMENT WHEN I WANT...

A GOOD RACLETTE

WHEN THE CRAVING TAKES ME, I ALWAYS FEEL LIKE IT'S BEEN AGES SINCE I LAST HAD ONE.

WELL...

I'LL MAKE ONE TONIGHT.

HAVE TO.

EVEN IF I ATE ONE, LET'S SAY, LAST NIGHT.

I DON'T KNOW ABOUT YOU, BUT I'M ALWAYS APPREHENSIVE ABOUT EATING RACLETTE AT SOMEONE ELSE'S PLACE.

I HOPE THE CHEESE STORE IS STILL OPEN!

IF THE SMALLEST DETAIL IS MESSED UP, IT CAN QUICKLY TURN INTO A NIGHTMARE...

HOW MANY OF US HAVE EXPERIENCED SOMETHING LIKE THIS:

Come on, live a little, there's at least one piece of sausage per person!

OR, EVEN WORSE, THIS:

SHARE WITH YOUR NEIGHBOR, THERE AREN'T ENOUGH COUPELLES FOR EVERYONE!

...

HOW MANY WERE VICTIMS OF:

I already made another dessert so I didn't make much.

DESPITE THAT, A GOOD RACLETTE ISN'T HARD TO DO RIGHT.

AND THAT ONE WITH THE GREEN PEPPER, TOO.

SOME OF THAT RAW MILK CHEESE...

HAHaha!!!

YOU JUST HAVE TO KNOW HOW!

THE TEN COMMANDMENTS OF RACLETTE

I. TOO MUCH TO EAT THERE WILL BE.

II. A GOOD CHEESE YOU MUST CHOOSE (OR PERHAPS SEVERAL).

III. ENOUGH CHARCUTERIE YOU WILL PROVIDE.

IV. ORGANIC POTATOES YOU WILL BUY.

V. A DRY WHITE WINE WILL ACCOMPANY YOUR MEAL.

VI. YOUR TOOLS YOU WILL CHOOSE

VII. THE APPROPRIATE SPICES YOU WILL PROVIDE

VIII. THE STAPLES YOU WILL NOT FORGET

IX. ONE COUPELLE MINIMUM PER PERSON YOU WILL DISTRIBUTE

X. BIG EATERS YOU WILL INVITE.

(1) DILUTE ONE TABLESPOON OF PEANUT BUTTER INTO CIDER VINEGAR OR BALASAMIC VINEGAR OR EVEN PRESSED LEMON.

(SOMETHING ACIDIC)

IN A BOWL LIKE THIS, OR ANOTHER

WITH PLENTY OF INGREDIENTS

...OR NOT!

APPLE BLACK RADISH SALAD

SUNFLOWER OIL

PEANUT BUTTER

SESAME SEEDS

APPLES

BALSAMIC VINEGAR

CIDER VINEGAR

BOWL

SQUASH SEEDS

A BLACK RADISH

LEMON

KATANA

PESTLE

GRATER

SUGAR

SALT

PEPPER

CUMIN

CURRY

CORIANDER

PEANUTS

PAN

GRAPESEED OIL

SPOON

(6) WANT TO MAKE THE WHOLE THING HARDER? ROAST THE SEEDS IN THE PAN:

SEEDS

NO FAT

VIGILANCE

SPICE WITH WHATEVER YOU HAVE LYING ABOUT AND SPRINKLE WITH SUGAR. WHEN IT'S GRILLED LET IT CARAMELIZE (WHEN THE SUGAR MELTS) AND...

I BURNED EVERYTHING!!!

(2) GRIP THE KATANA TIGHTLY IN ONE HAND AND THROW THE BLACK RADISH AND APPLES* INTO THE AIR WITH THE OTHER...

(* PEEL THEM BEFOREHAND.)

AND SLICE!

VERY THIN SLICES

WAUE!

IF YOU'RE NOT FEELING CONFIDENT, A GRATER IS FINE, TOO.

(2) ADD THE APPLES AND BLACK RADISH INTO THE BOWL YOU SAW IN (1).

(YEAH, YOU WOULD'VE BEEN BETTER OFF GETTING A LARGER SALAD BOWL.)

LET IT MACERATE FOR A MOMENT. THE RADISH WILL COOK IN THE COLD AND LOSE ITS STRENGTH:

WHAT ARE YOU DOING DAVE?

MY MIND IS GOING

(4) ADD SALT, PEPPER, AND GRAPESEED OR SUNFLOWER OIL--SOME SORT OF OIL.

DON'T PUT TOO MUCH IN THE SALAD BOWL OR IT'LL BE TOO GREASY.

AND VOILA

NORMALLY, YOU'RE READY TO GO.

(5) YOU WANT TO MAKE IT LOOK NICE? TAKE THE PESTLE AND CRUSH THE SALTED PEANUTS...

OR ADD SESAME OR SUNFLOWER SEEDS, ETC.

SO PRETTY

lon.

Pépé Roni's Good Advice: palate   n° 017

Don't confuse "training your pet"

and "training your palate."

BECAUSE ANYONE CAN MAKE MISTAKES!

Palate: your appreciation of taste and flavor

PARIS CITY, 2023

IN FRONT OF THE RESTAURANT **STAR PALACE**, THERE IS AN EVERGROWING CROWD AFTER TODAY'S INCREDIBLE DISCOVERY!

STAY CALM.

WARNING: REAL BULLETS.

STAY CALM.

IN EFFECT, THE CAPTURE OF A 650 POUND SPECIMEN FROM A BYGONE ERA, WHICH HAS SENT THE FOODIES OF THE WORLD INTO A PANIC... THE **STAR PALACE** MAY MAKE A PROFIT OF SEVERAL MILLION ROUPIDOLLARS... THE CROWD COULD BREAK OUT INTO A RIOT AT ANY MOMENT!

YOU KNOW... IT WAS A REAL CHALLENGE TO COOK THIS FUCKING BEAST!

I PLAYED IT VERY SIMPLE TO RESPECT THE CRAZY TASTE!

ANTONIN P., HEAD CHEF OF **STAR PALACE**

SURE, $1,400 FOR THE MENU IS EXPENSIVE BUT IT'S WORTH THE PRICE... LET ME REMIND YOU, IT'S THE **LAST** OF ITS KIND.

E. BESSON REPLICANT II, MINISTER OF THE ALLIANCE

LISTEN... AFTER MY 45TH BIRTHDAY THERE'S NOT MUCH TO LOOK FORWARD TO BEFORE DEATH, SO I WANTED TO TASTE IT ONE MORE TIME!

IT'S INCREDIBLE THERE'S STILL ANOTHER ONE!

INCREDIBLE, YES! HOW DID WE GET TO THIS POINT WITHOUT EVEN SEEING IT COMING? MANKIND IS CRAZY!

FRANCE, MARCH 2010

WHAT?!

NO WAY!

WUUUiii!!!

SO, IS IT TRUE, CAN I?

YOU **CAN**. I GOT THEM THIS MORNING.

WOO...

WOO...

FRESH

HOW MUCH?

2 LBS!

WAH! THIS IS THE BEST DAY OF MY LIFE!

POISS

RED... RED TUNA FROM THE MEDITERRANEAN?

ARE YOU MESSING WITH ME, OR WHAT?

IT'S FINE: WE **CAN**! BAH, DON'T YOU READ THE PAPERS? JAPAN AND QATAR ALREADY SAID THAT TUNA ISN'T ENDANGERED **AT ALL**!

AT ALL!

NOT AT ALL?

WE WERE WRONG!

PARIS CITY, 2023

CAN YOU BELIEVE THAT AT ONE TIME WE COULD HAVE AVOIDED ALL THIS... YOU KNOW, BACK WHEN THE INTERNET WAS STILL A THING, ALL IT TOOK WAS A COUPLE IDIOTS SAYING THAT TUNA WASN'T ENDANGERED, AND POOF! IT DISAPPEARED!

I DON'T KNOW WHERE THAT CAME FROM, BECAUSE TUNA HAS ALWAYS BEEN ENDANGERED.

OF COURSE, THE FAKE TUNA'S FINE, BUT THE TEXTURE JUST ISN'T THE SAME.

leon.

THE OTHER DAY, WHEN I WAS LEAVING MY HOUSE, I REALIZED THAT I HAD LOST MY GRANDPA.

I SEARCHED FOR HIM EVERYWHERE, UNDER MY FURNITURE, IN THE TRASH CAN, BEHIND THE COUCH: I JUST COULDN'T FIND MY GRANDPA.

I HAVE TO ADMIT I DIDN'T THINK ABOUT HIM ALL THE TIME, BUT BECAUSE HE WAS QUITE PRACTICAL AND VERY SMALL, I OFTEN CARRIED HIM WITH ME, IN ONE OF MY JACKET POCKETS.

I REMEMBER HE ALWAYS HAD GREAT ADVICE WHENEVER I WENT TO THE BUTCHER'S.

ARE YOU TALKING TO ME?

OH, NO.

THE STOMACH! BUY THE STOMACH!

DON'T TOUCH THE SAUSAGES.

OH WOW! LOOK AT ALL THAT TRIPE!

AND WHENEVER I WAS CHOOSING A WINE AT THE LAST MINUTE, I COULD COUNT ON HIM FOR ADVICE, EVEN IF HE OFTEN WENT BACK TO THE SAME BOTTLES.

BUY THE VISAN, I TELL YOU, BOY!

OR THE CROZES-HERMITAGE!

A CAIRANNE, THEN!

YOU'RE GOING TO LEAVE WITH A CÔTES-DU-RHÔNE ANYWAYS, THAT'S THE ONLY REAL WINE!

BUT GRANDPA... I NEED A WINE THAT GOES WITH FISH...

BECAUSE I WAS SAD TO HAVE LOST HIM, I DECIDED TO COOK MYSELF SOMETHING HE USED TO MAKE THAT I REALLY LOVED. HE'D MAKE IT EVERY THURSDAY AFTER COMING HOME FROM THE MARKETS.

IT'S KIND OF A GREASY DISH AND IT'S NOT THAT COMPLICATED, BUT IT WAS MY GRANDFATHER'S.

NOW, TIME FOR THIS RACK OF LAMB... WITH GARLIC AND PARSLEY!

IT'S A GOOD THING YOU NEVER JUST HEATED UP CANNED FOOD FOR ME, ISN'T IT GRANDPA?

(1) TO MAKE THIS DISH, YOU'LL NEED...

OLIVE OIL

SALT

PEPPER

HERBES DE PROVENCE

PARSLEY

GARLIC

RACK OF LAMB, IN PIECES, PREPARED BY THE BUTCHER.

(2) HEAT THE OIL (MY GRANDPA ALWAYS PUT AT LEAST A LITER) IN A PAN, BROWN THE LAMB, AND SPRINKLE WITH HERBES DE PROVENCE:

WHILE IT COOKS, PEEL AND SLICE TWO OR THREE CLOVES OF GARLIC (REMOVE THE STEM).

(3) CUT THE PARSLEY LEAVES AND CHOP THEM COARSELY:

WHEN THE LAMB IS ALMOST COOKED AND WELL GRILLED, THROW THE GARLIC INTO THE PAN, BROWN IT BEFORE SERVING IT, TOP WITH PARSLEY, SALT AND PEPPER: AND IT'S READY.

AND WHILE I WAS EATING THE LAMB, LIKE I USED TO, A TON OF MEMORIES CAME BACK TO ME AND I ALMOST CHOKED!

?

Hey! I can't believe this!

IT WAS MY GRANDPA! THERE HE WAS, PERCHED ON MY FORK: I WAS RELIEVED TO FIND HIM. MY LIFE COULD CONTINUE.

HAHAHA!

SURPRISE!

SO, KIDDO, YOU'RE COOKING RACK OF LAMB?

DID YOU USE ENOUGH OIL?

I HOPE YOU'RE HAVING A GOOD CHATE-ANEUF-DU-PAPE WITH IT!

Deglazing: diluting the caramelized juices at the bottom of a pan or a still-warm dish by adding a liquid in order to make a sauce.

Table of Recipes

Appetizers

Entrees

Desserts

Index

*Pépé Roni's Good Advice

Acknowledgments

At the beginning, Martin gave this project the impetus it needed to get started. Then Boris, Nicolas, Alexis, and Celia at *Le Monde* trusted me enough and that was a gift. Yannick believed in this project—he's a wonderful guy. Now Thierry, Nicolas, Caroline, Muriel, Sandrine, and Olivier at Gallimard are going above and beyond, and I hope to work with them for a long time to come.

The blog readers have been so supportive; I'm very lucky. Matthieu has a great place in Venice. Francois-Regis is truly charming. Katia and Yoann know Lausanne and vegetables, respectively, like the back of their hands. My mother still knows how to cook well and my *pépé* knew how to appreciate the pleasure of food. Celine always saves me at the end. Roland and I talk often—that means more than you think, believe me.

On the blog, talented authors generously gave their unedited stories: Anne Montel, Daniel Blancou, Dorothee de Monfreid, Frederik Peeters, Guillaume Plantevin, Greg Shaw, Hervé Bourhis, Lison Bernet, Leslie Plée, Louis-Bertrand Devaud, Martin Vidberg, Mathias Martin, Nancy Penna, Pochep, Terruer Graphique, Thibaut, Soulcie, one and two.

This book owes much to Florian. And Nancy is a really cool girl.

Thank you.

Bon Appétit